Yours Completely

HAVING A HEART THAT IS *Fully Devoted* TO GOD

By: Cindy Sue Baker

Yeomen Press
Box 281
Walton KS 67151
www.yeomenpress.com
yeomenpress@gmail.com

Fully *devoted*,
Wholly *true*,
Loyal forever,
Only to You.

Steadfast in love,
Faithful I'll be,
My heart is *committed*,
Yours completely.

Dedication

This book is dedicated to **WAYNE BURGER:**
my faithful friend, spiritual mentor, "adopted" dad,
occasionally an ornery burr in my saddle,
and a man who, for me, defines what it means
to be fully devoted to God.

Wayne, thank you for first planting the idea for this book
in my head one humid night in Vanuatu in 2010
as you challenged our mission team
to take a deeper look at the kings of the Divided Kingdom.
That study, and many others, is what makes you
an incredible teacher
because you are always able to lay out God's Word in a way
that is both understandable and awe-inspiring.

I love you!

Acknowledgements

Many thanks to **SHERRA JACKSON,** for her patient endurance in proof-reading this material. She was a great source of support, encouragement, and friendship along the way. And, of course, everyone needs a good friend to laugh with you (at you?) when you do crazy things... like spill a bowlful of Mod-Podge covered paintbrushes on the hotel carpet at Ladies Retreat.

As always, thank you to my best friend and husband, **AARON BAKER,** for knowing just what to say to push me along and for his loving support of all my writing endeavors. I'm sure I don't deserve him... and I mean that in the *good* way!

Table of Contents – *Yours* Completely

Chapter 1
What does it mean to be His Completely? ... page 1

Chapter 2 — King Saul
Being Completely Content ... page 9

Chapter 3 — King David
Having a Repentant Heart ... page 19

Chapter 4 — King Solomon
Having an Undivided Heart ... page 29

Chapter 5
The Divided Kingdom in a Nutshell ... page 37

Chapter 6 — King Rehoboam
Considering Your Influences ... page 45

Chapter 7 — King Jeroboam
Having a Heart that is God-Serving ... page 53

Chapter 8 — King Jehoshaphat
Taking Pride in the Ways of God ... page 65

Chapter 9 — King Ahab
Acquiring Spiritual Clarity ... page 77

Chapter 10 — King Hezekiah
Having a Heart that Trusts in God's Grace ... page 87

Chapter 11 — King Josiah
Having a Deep Love and Respect for God's Word ... page 101

CHAPTER 12 – CONCLUSION
What will be your Legacy? ... page 111

CHAPTER 13 – ADDITIONAL STUDY AIDS
Trivia of the Kings Review ... page 119
What does it mean to be Saved by Grace? ... page 120
5 Great Lessons from the Life of Hezekiah ... page 123

Copyright © 2016 by Yeomen Press
Box 281
Walton KS 67151
ISBN 978-0-9974209-0-6
Cover design by Jim L. Friesen
Printed in the U.S.A. by Mennonite Press, Inc.

INTRODUCTION — *Yours* COMPLETELY

HAVING A *Heart* THAT IS *Fully Devoted* TO GOD

Romans 15:4 says that "For whatever was written in earlier times was written for our instruction, so that through perseverance and the encouragement of the Scriptures we might have hope." By studying various kings of the Old Testament we will have the opportunity to learn what it means to be completely His. And in some cases, what it means to *not* be completely His. Each king we study will hopefully add something to our understanding of how to have a heart that is fully devoted to God.

At the beginning of each chapter you will find a section called "2 Minute Decompress". It is a known fact that deep breathing helps to calm the chaos of the mind. I know for me, personally, my mind gets going on the things I need to be doing for the day or problems in my life. When that happens I can read the words of an entire paragraph and not have a clue what it was about when I come to the end! And I have a feeling I am not alone! That said, I encourage you to take a few moments before each study to inhale and exhale slowly three times. It will help release your mind from its worldly cares so that you are better able to focus on the passage from God's Word or the words of the song printed for your deeper consideration.

You will find as you go throughout this study that I often use the terms "we" and "us". I include myself as one who has something to learn from this book, even as I write it. We all have our own individual struggles to overcome. That said, I call on each one of us to cut through the barriers of implied perfection, be real with yourself and be real with your sisters in Christ. Really, truly, whom are we kidding? Behind our matching clothes, flawless make-up, and shiny jewelry, we are all imperfect.

True confessions... I have this stubborn hair that grows randomly out of the middle of my forehead. Why? I have no idea. But, I do. It is my own personal reminder that I am not perfect. From that obnoxious little hair to the weaknesses and sins that I constantly battle in my life, I am just as blemished as the next gal. However, living with a complacent attitude towards my personal flaws and sometimes wayward heart is not good enough for me. I want to have a heart that is Completely and Fully Devoted to my God. And I hope you, too, desire to improve upon your own weaknesses. So, let us come together to learn, to grow and to help each other to reach our number one goal – heaven – by having a heart that is His Completely.

* All Scriptures are taken from the *New American Standard Bible* unless otherwise noted.

CHAPTER 1 - *Yours* COMPLETELY

WHAT DOES IT MEAN TO BE *His Completely*?

2 Minute Decompress – Breath slowly in and out three times. Then read and think about this verse in 2 Chronicles 16:9, "For the eyes of the Lord move to and fro throughout the earth, that He may strongly support those whose heart is completely His..."

From Ponder to Pen – Do you find it easier to show your devotion to God by obeying His commands or are you more readily moved by a deep, emotional love for Him? Why?

WHAT DRIVES YOUR DEVOTION?

It is my experience that most people tend to fall more to one side of the scale than the other. Some of us are task-driven. We see what needs to be done to obey God and we do it. We tend to be no-nonsense in our Christian walk and don't often find ourselves pulled this way and that by our emotions. For the most part, when faced with a challenge or particular situation, we see our choices as black and white. Others of us are emotionally-driven. We are often brought to tears (or at least an overwhelming sense of awe) at all that God has done for us. We worship with visible fervency and enthusiasm (and sometimes wonder at those who do not outwardly appear to be doing the same). While we see our choices as black and white, our emotional side makes it easier for us to consider the gray areas of a situation. Those of us who are task-driven have a hard time taking seriously those who are emotionally-driven. Those of us who

Chapter 1 – His Completely?

are emotionally-driven have a hard time understanding the intensity of those who are task-driven.

The above paragraph describes two very different types of Christians. Yet, each one, having been baptized into Christ, has put on Christ and is a viable member of the body of Christ. The task-driven Christian can become so focused on the necessity of obedience that they forget to engage their heart. The emotionally-driven Christian, if they are not careful, can easily build themselves a foundation of strong feelings rather than absolute truth. On either end of the spectrum they both have their strengths and weaknesses. Straying too far to one side or the other can result in shipwreck. However, striking a balance between each of these tendencies can result in the completeness that God is seeking to find in each of us.

LOYALLY HIS

So, what does all that have to do with being Completely His? To answer this question, let's look at this verse in 2 Chronicles 16:9 again, this time in the New King James Version. "For the eyes of the Lord run to and fro throughout the whole earth, to show Himself strong on behalf of those whose heart is loyal to Him…"

This version uses the word "loyal". Loyal is a word that we are familiar with. We use it to describe our love of our favorite sports team. We use it to describe a relationship between a husband and wife. We use it to describe Scruffy, our fearsome little Yorkie, that barks incessantly at every stranger it sees on the sidewalk. Those are examples of what it means to be loyal in human terms. According to the *Oxford American Dictionaries*, "Loyal" is described as: "giving or showing firm and constant support to a person or an institution".

It seems that "loyal" is a very fitting word to describe our relationship with God and His relationship with us. There is complexity to the different facets of our love for God and His love for us. Hebrew scholars Keil and Deilitch define this word as "wholly or undividedly given to the Lord".

2 CHRONICLES 16:9
NKJV – "loyal"
NASB – "wholly devoted"
NIV(1984) – "fully devoted"
ESV – "wholly true"
KJV – "perfect"
NIRV – "with all his heart"
E2R – "faithful"

Taking a brief look at different versions of the Bible can help paint a clearer picture of what certain words or phrases mean and the idea behind them. From the New American Standard Bible, New International Version (1984), English Standard Version, and New International Readers Version we gain the understanding that being loyal to God is something that should encompass our whole heart, not just a mere portion of our lives or a single day of our week. The King James Version goes the direction of "perfect", while the Easy-to-Read Version brings out the idea of faithfulness. Each of these versions bring a slightly different aspect to the word, helping us to understand the complexity of having a heart that is Completely His.

TAKING A CLOSER LOOK

Read the following verses. What do you notice about these kings and the Israelite people and their devotion to God?

1 KINGS 15:3 – "And he [Abijam] walked in all the sins that his father did before him, and his heart was not wholly true to the Lord his God, as the heart of David his father."

Chapter 1 – His Completely?

2 Kings 20:3 – "Remember now, O Lord, I pray, how I [Hezekiah] have walked before You in truth and with a loyal heart, and have done what was good in Your sight…"

1 Chronicles 29:9 – "Then the people [the Israelites] rejoiced, for they had offered willingly, because with a loyal heart they had offered willingly to the Lord; and King David also greatly rejoiced."

We can see from each of these verses that being loyal to God is something that takes place in the depths of our hearts and it is also something that is shown in our actions, in our obedience to God. Abijam walked in sin, Hezekiah walked in truth, the Israelites gave their offerings to God willingly. All of these are outward actions that revealed what was going on inside their hearts.

Is it important to God that we are completely devoted to Him? Over and over in His Word God tells us that it is! Read through the following verses taken from the New King James Version where the term "loyal" is used to describe this complete devotion to God:

1 Kings 8:61 - "Let your heart therefore be **loyal** to the Lord our God, to walk in His statutes and keep His commandments, as at this day."

1 Kings 11:4 – "For it was so, when Solomon was old, that his wives turned his heart after other gods; and his heart was not **loyal** to the Lord his God, as was the heart of his father David.

1 Kings 15:3 – "And he walked in all the sins of his father, which he had done before him; his heart was not **loyal** to the Lord his God, as was the heart of his father David."

1 Kings 15:14 – "But the high places were not removed. Nevertheless, Asa's heart was **loyal** to the Lord all his days."

2 KINGS 20:3 – " 'Remember now, O Lord, I pray, how I walked before You in truth and with a **loyal** heart, and have done what was good in Your sight.' And Hezekiah wept bitterly."

1 CHRONICLES 28:9 – "As for you, my son Solomon, know the God of your father, and serve Him with a **loyal** heart and with a willing mind; for the Lord searches all hearts and understands all the intent of the thoughts. If you seek Him, He will be found by you; but if you forsake Him, He will cast you off forever."

1 CHRONICLES 29:9 – "Then the people rejoiced, for they had offered willingly, because with a **loyal** heart they had offered willingly to the Lord; and King David rejoiced greatly."

1 CHRONICLES 29:19 – "And give my son Solomon a **loyal** heart to keep Your commandments and Your testimonies and Your statutes, to do all these things, and to build the temple for which I have made provision."

2 CHRONICLES 15:17 – "But the high places were not removed from Israel. Nevertheless the heart of Asa was **loyal** all his days."

2 CHRONICLES 16:9 – "For the eyes of the Lord run to and fro throughout the whole earth, to show Himself strong on behalf of those whose heart is **loyal** to Him…"

2 CHRONICLES 19:9 – "And he commanded them saying, 'Thus you shall act in the fear of the Lord, faithfully and with a **loyal** heart.'"

2 CHRONICLES 25:2 – "And he did what was right in the sight of the Lord, but not with a **loyal** heart."

Chapter 1 – His Completely?

> **BIBLE CLASS ACTIVITY**
>
> Divide into three groups. Give each group a blank sheet of paper with one of the following questions written at the top. Have each group list out ideas that seek to answer their assigned question.
>
> Group 1 – How can you tell that someone is obeying the Lord?
>
> Group 2 – How can you tell that someone loves the Lord?
>
> Group 3 – How can you tell that someone is loyal to God?
>
> Afterwards, share the answers that each group came up with. What do you notice about the answers as a whole? How are they similar or different?

Earlier we talked about two different types of Christians – those that are more task-driven and find it easier to be in obedience to Christ's commands and those that are more emotionally-driven and find it easier to be passionate about their life in Christ. Is one of these tendencies better than the other? Is it more important to show our loyalty to God by obeying Christ's commands or by engaging the emotions within our heart?

FINDING THE BALANCE

The Jews of the New Testament were often guilty of tipping the scales in favor of their desire to follow the letter of the law. They had trouble with the faith aspect of the New Covenant. They pushed and pushed circumcision, which was a rule of the Old Law, not the New Law. What did Paul say of their attempt to gain salvation through circumcision in Galatians 5:2-4? "Behold I, Paul, say to you that if you receive circumcision, Christ will be of no benefit to you. And I testify again to every man who receives circumcision, that he is under obligation to keep the whole Law. You have been severed from Christ, you who are seeking to be justified by law; you have fallen from grace."

In contrast there is also great spiritual danger in just going through the motions of our Christian walk, doing all the "right" things, but without engaging the heart. In Isaiah 29:13 the Lord rebukes the Israelites, "Because this people draw near with their words, and honor Me with their lip service, But they remove their hearts far from Me, And their reverence for Me consists of tradition learned by rote". Again in Revelation 2:4 Jesus admonishes the church in Ephesus, "But I have this against you, that you have left your first love."

Is the heart important when it comes to being completely devoted to God? Is our obedience to God's Word important when it comes to being completely devoted to God? Yes and Yes! We cannot be loyal to God without activating our heart any more than we can be loyal to God and not obey His commands. If we try to have one without the other, we find ourselves only partially devoted to Him.

Let us seek to find the harmony of our obedience and our heart. Both are necessary to be fully devoted to God, so that by our lives we can humbly say, "Almighty God, I am Yours Completely."

Chapter 1 – His Completely?

Questions for Further Study

1. What are some ways that God shows Himself strong on our behalf?

2. What are some things we tend to be loyal to in our lives? Who are some people we tend to be loyal to in our lives? Should our loyalty to these supersede our loyalty to God?

3. Compare and contrast having a loyalty to God versus having a loyalty to something other than God in light of how it affects our home life and children.

4. What similarities do you see between the examples of Abijam, Hezekiah, and the Israelites given in this chapter and those people listed in the "Hall of Faith" in Hebrews chapter 11?

CHAPTER 2 — *Yours* COMPLETELY

King Saul — HAVING A HEART THAT IS FULLY DEVOTED TO GOD MEANS:
Being Completely Content

2 Minute Decompress — Breath slowly in and out three times. Consider this verse in 1 Timothy 6:6 – *"But godliness actually is a means of great gain when accompanied by contentment."*

From Ponder to Pen — "Being Completely Content"… so much easier said than done, is it not? We all struggle to be truly happy with every circumstance in our lives. In what areas of your life do you struggle to be fully content with what you have?

KING SAUL'S STORY IS FOUND IN:

1 Samuel 8:1 and intertwines through the lives of the prophet Samuel and King David until Saul meets his end in 1 Samuel 31:13. Smatterings of Saul are mentioned in the early years of David's reign as the kingdom transfers from the lineage of Saul to the house of David.

Shortly after Saul is named king, God's prophet, Samuel, speaks to the people about their choice to have a king. Although God knows it will mean difficult times for His people, He allows them to have the king they so desperately desire. With this in mind Samuel calls the Israelite people to continue to follow God and seek after the things that have eternal value.

Chapter 2 – Being Completely Content

> *"Samuel said to the people, 'Do not fear. You have committed all this evil, yet do not turn aside from following the* Lord*, but serve the* Lord *with all your heart. You must not turn aside, for then you would go after futile things which can not profit or deliver, because they are futile' "* (1 Samuel 12:20-21).

How were they to do all that God would have them do and not turn aside to futile things? As the newly established leader of the Israelite people, it fell to King Saul to lead them in the way they should go. The way they were to go was in following the Lord and serving Him with all their heart. In the beginning, Saul seems to be humbled by his new position as king. He starts off well in his leadership by bringing the Ammonites to destruction, with the help of God.

Through King Saul we learn that contentment begins with humility. When King Saul humbled himself before God and sought to do God's will, he was happier and more content. However, in his later years as king he was not fully devoted to God and we see how his life became burdened by jealousy and strife.

In 1 Samuel 9:1 - 10:16 God shows Samuel His will for Saul to become king over Israel. In 1 Samuel 9:21 Saul shows his humble heart. He does not see himself as anything great. *"Am I not a Benjamite, of the smallest of the tribes of Israel, and my family the least of all the families of the tribe of Benjamin? Why then do you speak to me this way?"* As Samuel reveals God's will to Saul, he gives several rather detailed instructions for Saul to follow and Saul proves himself to have great potential as king over the Israelites in his willingness to follow all that Samuel tells him to do.

Nationwide Discontent

A lack of contentment was what got the Israelite people into trouble in the first place, even years before the time of Saul! In 1 Samuel 8:19-20 we see what is fueling their desire for a king.

> "Nevertheless, the people refused to listen to the voice of Samuel, and they said, 'No, but there shall be a king over us, **that we also may be like all the nations**, that our king may judge us and go out before us and fight our battles.'"

They weren't content with what God had given to them and all that He had done for them. They wanted to be just like everyone else. "Keeping up with the Joneses" at its worst! Throughout the course of the United Kingdom and by the end of the Divided Kingdom, we can see God's wisdom and warnings coming true as king after king leads Israel further from God. But, God told them it would be this way, didn't He? Look back at 1 Samuel 8:10-18.

> "So Samuel spoke all the words of the LORD to the people who had asked of him a king. He said, 'This will be the procedure of the king who will reign over you: he will take your sons and place them for himself in his chariots and among his horsemen and they will run before his chariots. He will appoint for himself commanders of thousands and of fifties, and some to do his plowing and to reap his harvest and to make his weapons of war and equipment for his chariots. He will also take your daughters for perfumers and cooks and bakers. He will take the best of your fields and your vineyards and your olive groves and give them to his servants. He will take a tenth of your seed and of your vineyards and give to his officers and to his servants. He will also take your male servants and your female servants and your best young men and your donkeys and use them for his work. He will take a tenth of your flocks, and you yourselves will become his servants. Then you will cry out in that

Chapter 2 – Being Completely Content

day because of your king whom you have chosen for yourselves, but the L<small>ORD</small> *will not answer you in that day.'"*

Why didn't Israel listen? Why couldn't they just be content with what they had? 1 Samuel 12:12 says that the root of their discontent was that they were not happy, grateful or content with having God as their king. They thought that the grass was greener on the other side. Isn't this one of Satan's most valuable tools? If He can deceive us into thinking that the grass is greener on the other side, then we will go in search of the things that might potentially bring about our eternal destruction. Satan often tempts Christians with more money (this I will use to increase my holdings), more possessions (because my storage room has some extra space in it), a new husband or wife (because mine isn't making me happy anymore), a different church (because this one isn't exciting enough), and the empty satisfactions that the world so readily provides. This struggle didn't start or end with King Saul. God's people spent the next three thousand years struggling to learn that the grass isn't greener on the other side. The grass is only greener where it's watered.

A P<small>RODUCT</small> <small>OF THE</small> P<small>EOPLE</small>

In some ways, Saul's downfall of pride and discontent are not surprising. After all, he is product of his people. The Israelite people weren't content with God as King. "Like all the deeds they have done since the day that I brought them up from Egypt even to this day – in that they have forsaken Me and served other gods..." (1 Samuel 8:8). They wanted a king they could see with their eyes. God gave them kings chosen and anointed by Him, but even with these they were not content. And as those kings moved further and further away from God and into idolatry, the people went with them.

It all sounds so bleak, doesn't it? Was there no hope? All hope was not lost – God always cares for His people! Although He did not want them to ask for a king, He granted their request. While He gave them a king, knowing that they would regret it in the future, He gave them hope if their king would lead them in following Him. He offered them contentment! All they had to do was reach out and take it by following Him. Following God with your whole heart, serving Him in truth and love, will *always* bring contentment.

> *"For the LORD will not abandon His people on account of His great name, because the LORD has been pleased to make you a people for Himself. Moreover, as for me, far be it from me that I should sin against the LORD by ceasing to pray for you; but I will instruct you in the good and right way. Only fear the LORD and serve Him in truth with all your heart; for consider what great things He has done for you"(1 Samuel 12:22-24).*

When Samuel finishes this discourse to the Israelites on God's plan for them, he ends with a warning that they might not choose wickedness because wickedness would end in the destruction of them and their king. In this speech he basically give an ultimatum: Be content or be swept away.

Being Content to Wait

In 1 Samuel 13 we read about the war with the Philistines. The Philistine army was comprised of a great many people: 30,000 chariots, 6,000 horseman and people "like the sand on the seashore". Just looking upon them brought terror to the Israelite people! The text says that the Israelites were trembling when looking upon them – you can almost feel their fear and the certainty of death in the air. But, God had promised to be with them, hadn't He? Didn't

Chapter 2 – Being Completely Content

God, in just six verses prior, instruct the Israelites to remember what He had done for them? How difficult our problems seem when that is all we can think about! But when we consider all that the Lord has done for us, when we see the victories He has given us over our problems in the past, how much easier it is to trust Him in the future!

For Saul, trusting God involved waiting. Samuel, the prophet of God, promised that he would come to Gilgal where Saul was (verse 8). If God's prophet promises to be somewhere at a time that he appoints in order that he might offer sacrifices to the Lord on their behalf, don't you think he is going to do it? I imagine on Day 1, 2 and 3 Saul's faith was strong. He probably truly believed Samuel was going to arrive on time. On day 4 his faith likely began to wane a bit. "Will he really come? He said he would come. But, will he really come?" By the time day 7 rolls around Saul has given up all hope. He is done with waiting. He wanted deliverance and he wanted it immediately! He didn't trust that Samuel would arrive before the day was over. He gave up waiting before God could even answer his prayers! Have you ever done that? Sometimes waiting is so very hard! But, what does God tell us of waiting?

> *"Yet, those who wait for the Lord*
> *Will gain new strength;*
> *They will mount up with wings like eagles,*
> *They will run and not get tired,*
> *They will walk and not become weary."*
> *(Isaiah 40:31)*

The strength is in the waiting. If we don't give up hope, but wait for God in our time of need, He *will* deliver us! It may not always be in the way we *think* He will deliver us, but He always offers us what we need to cope in any situation. Saul became weaker in faith because he gave up waiting. He wasn't content to let Samuel fulfill his promise.

He took matters into his own hands and set out to perform the burnt offerings and peace offerings in Samuel's place. It wasn't just his lack of patience that led him to sin, but he also had complete disregard for the law of the Lord. On top of all that, he wasn't content with his role as king. He was never called by God to offer sacrifices on behalf of the people. That was a work that Samuel was given to do. Saul was king. His job was to lead the people to follow God. His job was to set the example of respecting Samuel's role as the priest and to let Samuel carry out his work to the best of his ability. King Saul's job was to wait, to be content and to wait.

> ### SOMETHING FOR US TO LEARN?
> ### DO WE HASTEN TO "SACRIFICE THE BURNT OFFERINGS" WHEN THAT WAS NEVER A JOB WE WERE CALLED TO DO?
>
> *Women's roles are a hot topic these days in churches worldwide. What should women do or not do in the worship service? Where is their place in the leadership of the church? Sometimes when we see men not stepping up to the work God has given them, the temptation is to jump in and do it ourselves. Sometimes, like King Saul, we figure that we can do the work just as well as anyone, so why shouldn't we?*
>
> *A sober-minded look at 1 Samuel 13:8-14 tells us why we should not. God has always given His people specific roles to fill. Prophets had their work, Priests had theirs. His People had their roles and their Leaders had theirs. Elders have their work and deacons have theirs. Men have their roles and women have theirs. He Who Never Changes has always expected us to fill the roles we were called to fill, to do them well and be content in them. After all, God does know best, doesn't He?*
>
> *We may not always understand why He has chosen to give men and*

> women different roles in the church, but He has. The New Testament teaches us by command and example what roles we are called to fill. As women, we have many works to do within the Lord's church and they are important! We may not have been called to lead worship or to fill the role as shepherds of the flock. But, can we be content with that?
>
> May we heed the warning of the things that were given for our learning (Romans 15:4) and thoughtfully consider what Samuel had to say about Saul's choice to offer the sacrifices. "You have acted foolishly; you have not kept the commandment of the Lord your God..." Let us be content to do the work we have specifically been called to do and let God work out the rest.

COMPLETELY HIS, COMPLETELY CONTENT

In our lives, do we find it hard to wait? Do we want to take control of a situation before we give God time to work in it? How hard it is to be content sometimes, isn't it? Sometimes I could just grit my teeth in frustration because I can't see a solution to my problem as quickly as I would like. But, when I feel compelled to bust out and take control or tremble in fear that things will not ever be resolved, that is when I should stop my internal blustering and be content! When I remember that my God loves me, when I consider all He has done for me in the past, what reason have I not to be content to wait for Him? He is God! When I seek to love him with my whole heart and walk in His truth, I will be content. Because everything I am, everything I do from my work to my worship will be about pleasing Him and being fully devoted to Him. Completely His, completely content. What great gain!

QUESTIONS FOR FURTHER STUDY

1. Why is it so difficult to attain contentment with your life and then to continue to maintain that contentment?

2. What other events in Saul's life reveal a lack of contentment?

3. What do contentment and trusting God have in common?

4. Why do you feel it is so hard for women to be content with the more "behind the scenes" roles in the church?

5. How can we help our daughters and young girls in our congregations to be content with the role God has given them and find joy in it?

Chapter 3 – Having a Repentant Heart

CHAPTER 3 — *Yours* COMPLETELY

King David — HAVING A HEART THAT IS FULLY DEVOTED TO GOD MEANS:
Having a Repentant Heart

2 Minute Decompress — Breath slowly in and out three times. Read Psalm 51 - the Psalm of David when Nathan the prophet came to him, after he had gone in to Bathsheba.

> "For You do not delight in sacrifice,
> otherwise I would give it;
> You are not pleased with burnt offering.
> The sacrifices of God are a broken spirit;
> A broken and a contrite heart, O God,
> You will not despise."
> (vs. 16-17)

From Ponder to Pen — Consider the meaning of this statement: When there is great opportunity, there is great responsibility, and great accountability. What do you think this meant for the life of King David? What do you think it means for your own life?

KING DAVID'S STORY IS FOUND IN:

1 Samuel 16 (intertwining with the latter part of Saul's life) through 2 Samuel 24:25. Also from 1 Kings chapter 1 (intertwining with the introduction of his son, Solomon) through 1 Kings 2:11.

Chapter 3 – Having a Repentant Heart

Without a doubt King David was one of the great men of the Old Testament. H.H. Halley said of David, *"All in all, David was a grand character. He did some things that were very wrong, but for an oriental king, he was a most remarkable man. He was, heart and soul, devoted to God and the ways of God. In a world of Idolatry, and in a nation that was continually falling away into Idolatry, David stood like a rock for God. In every circumstance of life he went directly to God, in Prayer, in Thanks, or in Praise"* (Haley's Bible Handbook, 1962).

BECOMING GOD'S MEASURING STICK

When looking at David's life, it was difficult to narrow down what portion to focus on. There are just so many valuable lessons that can be taken from his life! How does one choose among them? From his courage before Goliath, to his bond of friendship with Jonathan, to his trials in dealing with King Saul, to his faith in God and victories in battle, to seeing the depths of his heart in the Psalms.

King David was an exceptional representation of what it means to follow God, and yet he was so very human that we can easily identify with his struggles. It is no wonder that throughout the Divided Kingdom, God places King David as the measuring stick to which all other kings would be compared. Many times we can almost see the question asked, "Did they measure up to David?" There was no greater honor for the kings of the Divided Kingdom than to have the words, "He did right in the sight of the Lord, according to all that his father David had done" following their name.

That statement would be the equivalent of it being said of us at the end of our life, "She did right in the sight of the Lord, according to all that her Savior Jesus Christ had done." Who wouldn't want that said about them?

Despite all the wonderful options to focus on from the life of David, nothing seems to show what it means to have a heart completely devoted to God more than his experience with Bathsheba. The story of David and Bathsheba found in 2 Samuel 11, and subsequent events, bring this high and mighty king down to a very human level. Maybe we haven't been caught in the throws of the same sins that David was (adultery, lies, conspiracy to murder), but we have *all* sinned and fallen short of the glory of God (Romans 3:23). None of us can stand before God and say any different. But, it is what David did following those sins that made all the difference and truly made him a man after God's own heart (Acts 13:22). King David shows us that having a heart that is fully devoted to God means having a repentant heart.

THERE GOES PETER COTTONTAIL…

When reading 2 Samuel 11:1-4 I can't help but wonder, "What kind of a woman bathes in plain view of everyone?" And then I remember that it wasn't so long ago (just a few years, in fact) that I was bathing in an open-air structure in a remote village in Vanuatu. While my structure had three walls and I hung a shower curtain on a piece of bamboo, the entire top was visible from above. While I was careful to check the trees before I started bathing, it was possible, that if one should desire, they could simply climb one of the nearby trees and spy on me without my knowledge in the middle of my cold-water bucket bath. It is possible that Bathsheba was not aware that David was watching her. Or maybe she was, maybe she had designs on the king whom her husband served. Bathsheba remains a puzzle to me, but that isn't really the point of this chapter…just a rabbit to chase for a moment.

Chapter 3 – Having a Repentant Heart

ON THE BRINK OF SPIRITUAL DEMISE

As for David, he knew what he was getting into. He knew that Bathsheba belonged to another man. He well knew God's law "If there is a man who commits adultery with another man's wife, one who commits adultery with his friend's wife, the adulterer and the adulteress shall surely be put to death" (Leviticus 20:10). Things were not looking good for King David, but by the grace of God, he and Bathsheba managed to escape being put to death (2 Samuel 12:13-14). Nonetheless, Bathsheba became pregnant with his child and David decided he had to fix this problem.

It wasn't just adultery that ensnared him, but to cover up his sin he chose to do everything within his power to get Bathsheba's husband, Uriah, to go home and sleep with her. When that didn't work, he made the deplorable decision to take Uriah out of the picture.

> "Now in the morning David wrote a letter to Joab and sent it by the hand of Uriah. He had written in the letter saying, 'Place Uriah in the front line of the fiercest battle and withdraw from him, so that he may be struck down and die' " (2 Samuel 11:14-15).

Pretty shoddy actions for a man of God, don't you think? What was he thinking? Not only did he make a plan for Uriah to be killed, but he made Uriah carry that written plan to Joab, for him to carry out. What would Uriah have felt like if he knew that in his own hands he was delivering a written betrayal against him by the very king he served?

By the end of the battle King David's plan worked to his desiring and Uriah died. Following a traditional period of mourning David took Bathsheba as his wife. However, during that time David didn't seem to have a change of heart for his actions. Reading further into

2 Samuel 12 we see that David's heart remained hardened and blinded to his own sin.

Falling before God

In 2 Samuel 12:1-4 God sent the prophet Nathan to King David in an effort to bring him back to the right path. Nathan uses a compelling story in hopes that it will give David some perspective on the mess he has created with his sin.

> "Then the LORD sent Nathan to David. And he came to him and said,
> 'There were two men in one city, the one rich and the other poor.
> The rich man had a great many flocks and herds.
> But the poor man had nothing except one little ewe lamb
> Which he bought and nourished;
> And it grew up together with him and his children.
> It would eat of his bread and drink of his cup and lie in his bosom,
> And was like a daughter to him.
> 'Now a traveler came to the rich man,
> And he was unwilling to take from his own flock or his own herd,
> To prepare for the wayfarer who had come to him;
> Rather he took the poor man's ewe lamb and prepared it for the man who had come to him.'"

Nathan's story had its desired result and in verse 5 we see that "David's anger burned greatly against the man." You can almost imagine the fury in his voice as he declared that the man deserved to die for his actions. This is a pivotal moment in King David's life. He has become so blinded by his own sin and greed, so consumed with his own wants and desires, disregarding the Word of God, that he cannot even see that the story is an allegory of his own sins!

Chapter 3 – Having a Repentant Heart

Have you ever found yourself in that position? I know I have. How easy it is to cast a harsh judgment on the sins of others, when we, ourselves, are often ensnared by the very same traps! Lies, lust, greed, wagging-tongues, hasty judgments, careless words, selfishness... these are all so easy to identify in others, and sometimes so hard to admit to in ourselves. These sins can manifest themselves in different ways in the lives of different women. I may not lust after the man next door, but my lust for more money in my bank account and more clothes in my closet can be just as consuming. I may not swear and curse at my children like the lady at the bus stop, but when I speak careless words of criticism to my husband I do just as much damage.

Look at 2 Samuel 12:7-8. God reminds David of all that He has done for him. Reading these verses I can't help but think of my own life, the countless blessings that God has given me, times He has delivered me from myself. And how have I often repaid Him for His lovingkindness?

> "Nathan then said to David, "You are the man! Thus says the Lord God of Israel, 'It is I who anointed you king over Israel and it is I who delivered you from the hand of Saul. I also gave you your master's house and your master's wives into your care, and I gave you the house of Israel and Judah; and if that had been too little, I would have added to you many more things like these!"

And then God lowered the boom. "Why have you despised the word of the Lord by doing evil in His sight? ... " (verse 9). God continued to reveal to David the depths of His knowledge of the things David had done.

This scenario brings to mind what I believe to be one of the most humbling passages of Scripture in the New Testament. Hebrews 4:12-13ESV, *"For the word of God is living and active, sharper than any two-*

edged sword, piercing to the division of soul and of spirit, of joints and of marrow, and discerning the thoughts and intentions of the heart. **And no creature is hidden from his sight, but all are naked and exposed to the eyes of him to whom we must give account."** Nothing can silence our excuses like those words. Our Great, Almighty God knows all and He sees all. Like David, standing before Him in the midst of our sin, what more can we say in our defense than to fall before God and humbly admit, "I have sinned against the Lord."

GETTING BACK UP

David realized the despair of his iniquity. He realized the magnitude of God's lovingkindness towards him. He remembered again the joy of trusting in God and the blessings of His forgiveness. How was he able to do all of this? Because he had a heart for repentance. Psalm 32 and Psalm 51 are both noted to be written following his sin with Bathsheba. Although, it is a bit lengthy, Psalm 32 is one of many of his psalms that sheds light on what made David a man after God's own heart and it shows us how King David was fully devoted to God.

> *"How blessed is he whose transgression is forgiven,*
> *Whose sin is covered!*
> *How blessed is the man to whom the* LORD *does not impute iniquity,*
> *And in whose spirit there is no deceit!*
>
> *When I kept silent about my sin, my body wasted away*
> *Through my groaning all day long.*
> *For day and night Your hand was heavy upon me;*
> *My vitality was drained away as with the fever heat of summer.*
> *Selah.*
> *I acknowledged my sin to You,*
> *And my iniquity I did not hide;*
> *I said, "I will confess my transgressions to the* LORD*";*

And You forgave the guilt of my sin. Selah.
Therefore, let everyone who is godly pray to You in a time when You may be found;
Surely in a flood of great waters they will not reach him.
You are my hiding place; You preserve me from trouble;
You surround me with songs of deliverance. Selah.

I will instruct you and teach you in the way which you should go;
I will counsel you with My eye upon you.
Do not be as the horse or as the mule which have no understanding,
Whose trappings include bit and bridle to hold them in check,
Otherwise they will not come near to you.
Many are the sorrows of the wicked,
But he who trusts in the LORD, lovingkindness shall surround him.
Be glad in the LORD and rejoice, you righteous ones;
And shout for joy, all you who are upright in heart."

Because of his repentant heart, King David's walk with God did not end with the story of Bathsheba. He went on to do many great and wonderful things to help establish the kingdom of Israel. He shaped the Israelite people in such a way that his faithfulness would be lauded for generations to come.

It works the same way with us. You may find yourself caught in a sin that you find it hard to overcome. But, all is not lost. It may be a sin that consumes every thought in your mind. It may be a sin that that has deceived you into thinking that it really isn't that big of deal. It may be a sin that has led you down a path you do not want to go. It may be a sin that will have short-term consequences or one that you will feel the repercussions of long into the future. It may be a sin that has taken precedence over your home and family, work with the church, or fellowship with your Christian brothers or sisters. The list could go on and on because Satan is on the prowl looking for someone he might devour. We all find ourselves ensnared by things that are displeasing to God. But along with that there are choices facing us too. We can succumb to the temptations, be they little or big, or we can turn and fight.

1 Corinthians 10:13 reminds us that *"No temptation has overtaken you but such as is common to man; and God is faithful, who will not allow you to be tempted beyond what you are able, but with the temptation will provide a way of escape also, so that you will be able to endure it."* God is faithful. He is calling us to repentance, calling us to come back to Him, to find a better way, to re-focus our lives on His will and His Word.

WHAT WILL YOU CHOOSE TO DO?

I have made many choices in my life. What will I do with the life I have been given? What will I do with the lessons I have learned from my mistakes? What will I do with my opportunities, knowing I have often failed to take advantage of some of those opportunities in the past? What will I do with those horrid times I've come through? Will they make me bitter or will they make me stronger? What will I do with my blessings? Will I live in such a way that my gratefulness to God is evident to the world? Will I settle for living in my sin or will I fall on my knees in repentance? When there is great opportunity, there is great responsibility and great accountability. What will I choose? What will you?

Chapter 3 – Having a Repentant Heart

QUESTIONS FOR FURTHER STUDY

1. What opportunity have you been given in your life? What responsibilities do you find accompany that opportunity?

2. How does it make you feel to know that God sees all you do, hears all you think, knows the very depths of your heart?

3. Psalm 32:3 says, *"When I kept silent about my sin, my body wasted away through my groaning all day long."* Why does keeping silent about our sin have this affect upon us?

4. In contrast, Psalm 32:5-7 offers us hope. In what way does this verse give us hope?

5. What sin do you find yourself too quick to condemn in others, but sometimes rears its ugly head in your life?

CHAPTER 4 — *Yours* COMPLETELY

King Solomon — HAVING A HEART THAT IS FULLY DEVOTED TO GOD MEANS:
Having an Undivided Heart

2 Minute Decompress — I have this song written on the inside cover of my Bible. It has been so many years since I wrote it in there, I cannot even remember where I found it in the first place. But, I love the words well written by Steve Green (2006). Breath slowly in and out three times, then read and ponder these lines:

> "Oh, may all who come behind us find us faithful.
> May the fire of our devotion light their way.
> May the footprints that we leave lead them to believe.
> And the lives we live inspire to obey.
> Oh, may all who come behind us find us faithful."

From Ponder to Pen — If your life was being examined by the footprints that you leave, where would someone find you heading? Where have you been and where are you going, both in your physical life and in your spiritual life? Is it somewhere that inspires obedience in others? Will those who come behind you find you faithful?

Open your Bible and take a walk on back to Deuteronomy 17:14-15. Moses is giving the law and God knows that one day Israel will ask for a king. The people might not believe that it will happen, but God knew that it would happen because they would wish to be just like all

Chapter 4 – Having and Undivided Heart

the nations who were surrounding them. Keeping up with the Joneses ... again! God knew the trouble it would bring, but He was willing to let it happen so long as He was the one who did the choosing. But, when the time came, there were going to be some rules in place for the king. However, time, forbidden love, and sinfulness went to work on the heart of King Solomon and he managed to do every single thing that God had said not to do. And what we see is that a divided heart will result in a divided kingdom.

GOD SAID:	SOLOMON DID:
He shall not multiply horses for himself (Deuteronomy 17:16)	He multiplied horses for himself (1 Kings 10:26, 28)
He shall not multiply wives for himself (Deuteronomy 17:17)	He multiplied wives for himself (1 Kings 11:1-8)
He shall not increase silver and gold for himself (Deuteronomy 17:17)	He increased his wealth (1 Kings 10:23-29)
He shall write for himself a copy of the law and read it all the days of his life (Deuteronomy 17:18-19)	He turned away from God and God's law and took the people with him (1 Kings 11:9-10)

STARTING OFF ON THE RIGHT HEART

King David left behind a legacy of faithfulness to God when he died. He wasn't perfect, but he had a repentant heart for the times when he did sin. He taught us how to truly have a heart that is faithful to God. As a result, the kingdom of Israel was strong under his rule.

Before his death he spoke these words of instruction and encouragement to his son Solomon in 1 Kings 2:1-4.

> "As David's time to die drew near, he charged Solomon his son, saying, "I am going the way of all the earth. Be strong, therefore, and show yourself a man. Keep the charge of the Lord your God, to walk in His ways, to keep His statutes, His commandments, His ordinances, and His testimonies, according to what is written in the Law of Moses, that you may succeed in the all that you do and where ever you turn, so that the Lord may carry out His promise which He spoke concerning me, saying, "If your sons are careful of their way, to walk before Me in truth with all their heart and with all their soul, you shall not lack a man on the throne of Israel."

In his charge to Solomon, David told him the secret to having a united kingdom. He knew what it would ultimately take – the heart of the king must be a heart that is completely devoted to God.

KING SOLOMON'S STORY IS FOUND IN:

1 Kings 2:1–11:41 and in 1 Chronicles 22:1–29:28 and continuing into 2 Chronicles 1:1–9:31

Solomon began his rule on the right foot, with great humility of heart. He was so desirous of pleasing God that when God inquired of the one thing Solomon wanted most, he asked for an understanding heart. How far this humility would have carried him in his lifetime if he had just continued with his desire to do what was right and pleasing to God! King Solomon continued to seek to please the Lord in the early years of his reign. He loved God so much that he built a temple that was overflowing with splendor! Even as we watch movies and TV shows about the extravagant homes of celebrities today, it would seem that none of them could compare to the size or

Chapter 4 – Having and Undivided Heart

majesty of the temple of the Lord! He filled the structure with the finest materials: cedar, olive wood, cast metal, bronze, silver, gold, gold and more gold!

In 1 Kings 8:22-53 Solomon prays a lengthy prayer to God. This prayer reveals King Solomon's desire for himself and the Israelite people to serve God with their whole heart. In this prayer Solomon recognizes how easily man can fall into sin if he is not careful. Over and over he pleads with God to hear the prayers of the people, forgive them when they fall short of His will, and "teach them the good way in which they should walk" (8:36). Solomon concludes this time of dedication of the temple with a blessing to the Lord. This blessing sums up how Great our God is and all the amazing and wonderful things that are in His power to do for us if we will have a heart that is completely His! It may be a little bit of a lengthy blessing, but this one found in 1 Kings 8:56-61 is worth our time to read, ponder, and apply to our lives.

> "Blessed be the Lord, who has given rest to His people Israel, according to all that He promised; not one word has failed of all His good promise, which He promised through Moses His servant. May the Lord our God be with us, as He was with our fathers; may He not leave us or forsake us, that He may incline our hearts to Himself, to walk in all His ways and to keep His commandments and His statutes and His ordinances, which He commanded our fathers. And may these words of mine, with which I have made supplication before the Lord, be near to the Lord our God day and night, that He may maintain the cause of His servant and the cause of His people Israel, as each day requires, so that all the peoples of the earth may know that the Lord is God; there is no one else. Let your heart, therefore, be wholly devoted to the Lord our God, to walk in His statutes and to keep His commandments, as at this day" (1 Kings 8:56-61).
>
> Amen.

HOLDING FAST TO THE WRONG THINGS

Things started off so well for King Solomon. He sought wisdom from the Lord. He desired for himself and the Israelite people to love and serve God with a whole heart. It seems that he intended to be a man after God's own heart just as his father, David, was. There is a famous saying, "The road to hell is paved with good intentions". How true this was for King Solomon. Is it wrong to have good intentions? Of course not! Every good work begins with good intentions. But, it is what you do from that point on that paves the way for what is to come. King David tried to convey this teaching to his son Solomon before he died.

> *"As for you, my son Solomon, know the God of your father, and serve Him with a whole heart and a willing mind; for the Lord searches the hearts, and understands every intent of the thoughts. If you seek Him, He will let you find Him; but if you forsake Him, He will reject you forever"* (1 Chronicles 28:9).

Solomon had good intentions, but instead of carrying them out during the course of his reign we see a major problem develop in 1 Kings chapter 11. And it all begins with the words, "Now King Solomon loved many foreign women..." (you can almost hear the 'dum-dum-DUM!' ominously playing in the background).

God knew what would happen if the Israelite people became romantically entangled with people from other nations. He warned them of it, "You shall not associate with them, nor shall they associate with you, for they will surely turn your heart away after their gods", but King Solomon did not listen and he "held fast to these in love" (1 Kings 11:2). Verses 3 and 4 go on to say just how many "loves" Solomon had: 700 wives and 300 concubines (I can't even begin to comprehend what that was like!). And the result was

Chapter 4 – Having and Undivided Heart

just as God had promised. His wives turned his heart away from God and he ceased from being fully devoted to Him. What a tragic end to a man who had so much potential in the beginning! He had the best of everything PLUS understanding, and yet, instead of letting his head lead him in wisdom he allowed his heart to lead him in folly. His heart was divided between his love for God and his love for foreign women. We can see who won out in the end.

Why did he allow this to happen? What was the turn of events that led to this change? Solomon gave his heart away a little piece at a time and gradually fell away from God's way. Maybe each time it didn't seem like that big of deal, but over time there was less and less of his heart to give to God. He had divided it into too many pieces till there was nothing left for God.

Do we do that in our lives? Maybe we aren't giving our hearts away to foolish "love", or maybe we are - one "harmless" flirtation at a time. Maybe we give ourselves to our jobs. Love for the work we do is a blessing from God, but it isn't meant to consume our life and our time to the point that our responsibilities at work take precedence over our work with Christ's church or our duty to our families. Or maybe we divide our hearts amongst our secular interests: exercise clubs, crafting groups, our kid's ball games, filling our schedule with what we tell ourselves are worthwhile pursuits. It's just one ball game. It's just one missed worship service. It's just that our craft group can't meet any other night but Wednesday. But to what end? If it takes us away from our church family and our worship to God then how will it benefit us on the Last Day?

For Solomon, a divided heart resulted in a divided kingdom, a fraction of what could have been the whole. For you and me today a divided heart will result in a divided faith, a fraction of what could be a life that is His Completely.

Questions for Further Study

1. How would having a heart of understanding benefit you in your life?

2. What were the consequences that came because Solomon did not write a copy of the law and read it all the days of his life, as God instructed the kings to do in Deuteronomy 17:18-19?

3. How might it affect our lives if we ceased to read God's Word?

4. What things in your life press you to divide your devotion to God? What are some ways you can keep that from happening?

Chapter 5 – The Divided Kingdom in a Nutshell

CHAPTER 5 — *Yours* COMPLETELY

The Divided Kingdom
IN A NUTSHELL
(Some kings were nuttier than others...)

We can study all day long on the kings of the Old Testament in conjunction with the why and wherefore of having a heart that is loyal to God, but it is also a great opportunity to glean some understanding of Bible history along the way. Our faith can deepen only so far if we only seek to understand what is obvious. To really grow, stretch, and understand we need to challenge ourselves to dip below the surface.

So, in order to make the most of our study of the lives of the Kings that we will be studying in the following chapters, we need to get a better idea of what was going on in the world at the time of the Divided Kingdom.

FAST FACTS ABOUT THE DIVIDED KINGDOM

- This all takes place from roughly 1 Kings 12 – 2 Kings 11, as well as 2 Chronicles chapters 10 – 23.
- In 1 Kings 11:29-40 the prophet Ahijah foretold the Word of the Lord concerning the division of the kingdom of Israel. Verses 29-33 read as follows:

"It came about at that time, when Jeroboam went out of Jerusalem, that the prophet Ahijah the Shilonite found him on the road. Now Ahijah had clothed himself with a new cloak; and both of them were alone in the field. Then Ahijah took hold of the new

Chapter 5 – The Divided Kingdom in a Nutshell

cloak which was on him and tore it into twelve pieces. He said to Jeroboam, 'Take for yourself ten pieces; for thus says the Lord, the God of Israel, 'Behold, I will tear the kingdom out of the hand of Solomon and give you ten tribes. (but he will have one tribe, for the sake of My servant David and for the sake of Jerusalem, the city which I have chosen from all the tribes of Israel), because they have forsaken Me, and have worshiped Ashtoreth the goddess of the Sidonians, Chemosh the god of Moab, and Milcom the god of the sons of Ammon; and they have not walked in My ways, doing what is right in My sight and observing My statutes and My ordinances, as his father David did."

- While the kingdom was united (in the time of Kings Saul, David and Solomon) it went by the name of Israel.
- After the division (during the time of King Rehoboam – Solomon's son) it was split into two kingdoms: Israel (made up of 10 northern and eastern tribes) and Judah (made up of 2 southern tribes).

- **ISRAEL**
    - The larger of the two kingdoms comprised 10 tribes.
    - Made its mark in history by every single one of its 19 kings falling victim to corruption and sin during the time of their rule.
    - The first king, Jeroboam, who we will study in more depth later, set the tone for the rebellion from God that would constantly be a nasty mark on the pages of history for the kingdom of Israel.
    - In contrast to David, who was the measuring stick of righteousness in the eyes of God during the time of the United Kingdom, Jeroboam was at the opposite end of that measuring stick because of his sinful ways. Thus, we

often read the words, "For he walked in all the way of Jeroboam son of Nebat and in his sin which he made Israel sin, provoking the Lord God of Israel..." (1 Kings 16:26). As a result, Israel was constantly following their leaders into sin.
- Eventually, Israel was overcome and taken away into Assyrian captivity. Their sin as a nation contributed to their reign of power coming to a final end in 722BC. That is some serious food for thought! "Righteousness exalts a nation, but sin is a disgrace to any people" (Proverbs 14:34).

- **JUDAH**
  - The smaller of the two kingdoms was made up of two tribes (Judah and Benjamin).
  - While it had 19 kings, as well, not every king was bad. Some of Judah's kings were good and helped the Israelite people to remain faithful to God.
  - All of its kings were descendants of David.
  - The center of organized government and place of worship remained in Jerusalem, which fell in the territory of Judah. This probably helped to contribute to a more civilized society overall, as compared to Israel.
  - An alliance with King Ahab of Israel made a significant gash in Judah's history. Ahab, being a very corrupt king, introduced all kinds of idolatry to the people of Judah and created further separation between them and their God (Isaiah 59:2).
  - The kingdom of Judah was taken away into captivity by Babylon in 586BC (about 130 years after Israel met its end).

Chapter 5 – The Divided Kingdom in a Nutshell

- However, as promised by God, He preserved a remnant to return to the land and re-establish themselves as followers of God. This remnant would make a way for the line of David to continue until the promised birth of Jesus Christ, who would establish the spiritual kingdom, His church, a kingdom that will *never* end (Matthew 16:18).

DIVIDING THE NUT

Kings of Israel (922BC to 722BC)

WHO	REIGNED	LEGACY?
Jeroboam (Dynasty*)	22 years	Bad
Nadab	2 years	Bad
Baasha (Dynasty)	24 years	Bad
Elah	2 years	Bad
Zimri (Dynasty)	7 days	Bad
Omri/Tibni (Dynasty)	12 years	Terrible
Ahab	22 years	The Worst
Ahaziah	2 years	Bad
Jehoram (Joram)	12 years	Mostly Bad
Jehu (Dynasty)	28 years	Mostly Bad
Jehoahaz	17 years	Bad
Jehoash (Joash)	16 years	Bad
Jeroboam II	41 years	Bad
Zechariah	6 months	Bad
Shallum (Dynasty)	1 month	Bad
Menahem (Dynasty)	10 years	Bad
Pekahiah	2 years	Bad
Pekah (Dynasty)	20 years	Bad
Hoshea (Dynasty)	9 years	Bad

Kings of Judah (922BC to 586BC)

Who	Reigned	Legacy?
Rehoboam	17 years	Mostly Bad
Abijah	3 years	Mostly Bad
Asa	41 years	Good
Jehoshaphat	25 years	Good
Jehoram (Joram)	8 years	Bad
Ahaziah	1 year	Bad
Athaliah (Queen)	6 years	Terrible
Joash (Jehoash)	40 years	Mostly Good
Amaziah	29 years	Mostly Good
Uzziah (Azariah)	52 years	Good
Jotham	16 years	Good
Ahaz	16 years	Bad
Hezekiah	29 years	Very Good
Manassah	55 years	Terrible
Amon	2 years	Terrible
Josiah	31 years	Very Good
Johoahaz (Joahaz)	3 months	Bad
Jehoiakim (Eliakim)	11 years	Bad
Jehoiachin (Jeconiah)	3 months	Bad
Zedekiah (Mattaniah)	11 years	Bad

* For those of you who are as unclear as I was as to what constitutes a Dynasty...a Dynasty is a succession of rulers from the same family. However, you will note that a few times the Dynasty was started and ended with just one King. That's what we call an Epic Fail.

Each of the kings listed above left a legacy behind when they died. History does not lie and they were known by their actions as being a very good king or a very bad king. Along with the pages of our Bible, this study will seek to paint a picture of what each king was like and if they had a heart that was loyal to God.

Exactly as God had Promised

In Acts 27 the apostle Paul is on a ship that is facing destruction. However, God promises Paul that he and the other men will not lose their lives so long as they do what He tells them. In verse 25 Paul says, "Therefore keep up your courage, men, for I believe God that it will turn out exactly as I have been told." And it did.

God does not lie. He said there would be a division of the kingdom in 1 Kings chapter 11 and it came about just as God had said. I imagine Jeroboam may have scoffed a bit at the idea, after all he was not a follower of God. However, time passed, events happened, choices were made, and the kingdom divided from the hand of King Rehoboam. And it all happened exactly as the Lord had promised. Yet, in all of the division and corruption that came to pass in the years following, God never forgot His people. He never let go of His plan to save them from their sins. When the remnant returned to Jerusalem, the faith of the Israelite people was renewed and their hearts turned back to God.

Interestingly, if you remember one of the things that King Solomon did not do that God said he must do was to "read and study the law of the Lord all the days of his life" (Deuteronomy 17:18-19). Solomon's departure from God's Word set the stage for his disloyalty to God. But when the remnant returned to Jerusalem, they were led by a priest named Ezra who had set himself apart because he was well versed in the law of Moses. Ezra 7:6 says that "the king granted him all he requested because the hand of the Lord his God was upon him [Ezra]." Isn't that what God promised in 2 Chronicles 16:9? "The eyes of the Lord move to and fro throughout the earth that He may strongly support those whose heart is completely His..."

Why was God's hand upon Ezra? "For Ezra had set his heart to study the law of the Lord and practice it, and to teach His statutes and ordinances in Israel" (Ezra 7:10). This is the very thing that Solomon did not do! Ezra showed himself to have a heart that was fully devoted to God. He would help lead the Israelite people to remain faithful to God so that God could work His plan for the redemption of His people, just as He had promised.

Despite the ups and downs of the time of the kings, God still brought Jesus Christ into this world for the salvation of our souls and the redemption of His people. He has been faithful and it has all turned out just has He had promised. If that is not a reason to devote your heart to being Completely His, I do not know what is.

Chapter 5 – The Divided Kingdom in a Nutshell

QUESTIONS FOR FURTHER STUDY

1. What other promises has God made to us that we can count on?

2. What is the effect on a nation when there is a succession of godless leaders?

3. What are some ways our nation has been negatively affected by our leaders in the last 100 years?

4. What are some ways our nation has been positively affected by our leaders in the last 100 years?

5. What are some practical ways we can set our hearts to know God's Word?

Chapter 6 — *Yours* Completely

King Rehoboam — Having a Heart that is fully Devoted to God means:
Considering Your Influences

2 Minute Decompress — Breath slowly in and out three times. Then read and think about these verses in Psalm 1:1-3.

> "How blessed is the man who does not
> walk in the counsel of the wicked,
> Nor stand in the path of sinners,
> Nor sit in the seat of scoffers!
> But his delight is in the law of the Lord,
> And in His law he meditates day and night.
> He will be like a tree firmly planted by streams of water,
> Which yields its fruit in its season
> And its leaf does not wither;
> And in whatever he does, he prospers."

From Ponder to Pen — In the past, who has influenced you to make a bad or foolish decision? What did it cost you? How will you keep it from happening again?

King Rehoboam's story is found in:
1 Kings 12:1-15 and 2 Chronicles 10:1–12:16

Chapter 6 – Considering Your Influences

Crack that Spine!

When my youngest daughter, Melia, was about two years old she was really into watching *Richard Scarry's Busy Town Mysteries* on DVD. In an effort to train children to ask the six most important questions you can ask to learn more about a situation, each episode had the catchiest little song that they chanted to beat: "Who, What, Why and How? Who, What, When, Where, Why and How?"

So, in this chapter we are going to take a slightly different approach in order to learn more about King Rehoboam by asking those all-important questions: "Who, What, Why and How? Who, What, When, Where, Why and How?"

This is an open Bible study, so first, let's read the passage of 2 Chronicles 9:31 - 10:19. Once you have read through these verses, answer the following questions and see what King Rehoboam's life has to do with having a heart that is fully devoted to God.

Who are the main people or group that this passage is about?

When did all this happen?

Where did all this happen?

What did Israel request of King Rehoboam?

Who did Rehoboam consult with the first time he sought advice?

WHY did he seek the advice of the elders?

WHAT did the elders tell him?

WHY did Rehoboam consult with the young men?

WHAT did the young men tell him?

HOW did Rehoboam answer Israel?

THE EFFECTS OF BAD COMPANY

Saint Augustine said "Bad company is like a nail driven into a post, which, after the first and second blow, may be drawn out with little difficulty; but being once driven up to the head, the pincers cannot take hold to draw it out, but which can only be done by the destruction of the wood."

Thus it was with King Rehoboam. Might he have used a little wisdom and saw the error that his contemporaries were leading him to, he could have saved the kingdom. However, foolishness, selfishness, and just plain idiocy prevailed, effectively driving the nail up to the head. By the time Rehoboam met with the elders and his spiritual advisors, he had already made up his mind who he was going to allow to influence him. And the only hope for Israel's future was the destruction of the wood.

From this passage in 2 Chronicles 9:31-10:19 we can see that who we allow to influence us matters! Our influences have a direct impact on having a heart that is loyal to God. Those people (and sometimes things, activity, habits) we allow to influence us will either help us to grow stronger in faith or they will lead us away from God. But, it is our choice.

Determined to Disobey?

The reality is that God will allow people who are determined to disobey Him continue on the path that their heart is set on. Romans 9:17 speaks of Pharaoh in the time of the Old Testament. Pharaoh was so determined to destroy the Israelites and to disobey God that God gave him over to that. "For the Scripture says to Pharaoh, 'For this very purpose I raised you up, to demonstrate My power in you, and that My name might be proclaimed throughout the whole earth". Did God want that for Pharaoh? Of course not! God desires for all men everywhere to be saved and to come to a knowledge of the truth (1 Timothy 2:4). However, God gives us free will. He will not force anyone to do what is right, not even the King of Egypt.

If you think about it, it is almost scary - to think of how often I am the one with the stubborn heart. How often do I fall down in my Christian walk and seem determined to continue practicing the sin I hate? Who am I to say at what point God will give me over to my sin as He gave over Pharaoh to his idolatry or the Gentiles to their degrading passions (Romans 1:26)? Sometimes we are guilty of consoling ourselves that "Well, I have never done anything *that* bad!" And yet, all sin separates us from God, and all sin keeps us from having a heart that is His Completely.

In 1 Kings 11:29-38 it was prophesied by God that the kingdom would divide. This seems to be what it means in I Kings 12:15 when it says that, "So the king did not listen to the people, for it was a turn of events from God that the Lord might establish His word, which He spoke through Ahijah the Shilonite to Jeroboam son of Nebat." God knew that Rehoboam's rebellion would lead to the divided kingdom. He didn't force Rehoboam to do what he did, God simply knew that it would happen. He even gave Rehoboam the opportunity to choose what was right. God provided him with a council of elders who were ready and willing to lead him in a better way. But, like Pharoah who disregarded God's opportunities to let the Israelite people go, Rehoboam remained obstinate and did exactly what he wanted to do. This occurrence reminds us once again that if we are determined to forsake God and follow our own will, He will not stop us.

Are you Unevenly Yoked?

2 Chronicles 10:14 speaks about the yoke that was upon the Israelite people while they were under the rule of both King Rehoboam and his father, King Solomon. While a yoke is used to describe something that is heavy and burdensome, it also holds another meaning. The purpose of a yoke is to bind two animals together that they might move in the same direction to accomplish a specific goal. In this way a yoke is a means of discipline. Often times we read of yoking two oxen together to plow a field. That is usually the image I see in my head when thinking about a yoke. There is a valuable lesson to learn from the yoke. If you yoke yourself to someone who is influencing you to do things that are against God's will and His Word, how will that affect your life? Every cause has an effect. Rehoboam yoked himself to his contemporaries, allowing them to influence the decisions that he made as a ruler. Look at what the effect was!

Chapter 6 – Considering Your Influences

2 Chronicles 10:13 says, "The king answered them harshly, and King Rehoboam forsook the counsel of the elders. He spoke to them according to the advice of the young men…". Rehoboam chose whom he wanted to listen to. That advice cost him his head of forced labor (vs. 18) at the hands of the people who stoned him to death. And ultimately an even greater result came of his choice, "So Israel has been in rebellion against the house of David to this day" (vs. 19).

If we want to be women who have hearts that are completely devoted to our God, we must take into account who or what is influencing us. We may think on the surface that the two have nothing to do with each other, but from the life of King Rehoboam we can easily see that if we fail to consider the people and activities we surround ourselves with, it can lead to foolish choices. Those foolish choices can have heavy consequences. So, let's strive for better!

Ephesians chapter 5 begins with wisdom of how we ought to conduct ourselves in the world around us. "Therefore be imitators of God, as beloved children, and walk in love, just as Christ also loved you and gave Himself up for us, an offering and sacrifice to God as a fragrant aroma" (Ephesians 5:1-2). Verses 3-4 encourage us, as Christians, to seek those things that are pleasing to the Lord and offers several examples of things that are pleasing and things that are not. This passage shows us how to be loyal to God and verses 15-17 include a gentle warning, "Therefore be careful how you walk, not as unwise men but as wise, making the most of your time, because the days are evil. So then do not be foolish, but understand what the will of the Lord is."

If we can shed ourselves of bad influences in our lives and seek to understand what the will of the Lord is, we will be well on our way to cultivating a heart that is His Completely.

QUESTIONS FOR FURTHER STUDY

1. Who do you find yourself yoked to in your life? Are they leading you closer to God or further from Him?

2. Give some examples of people that we have no choice but to be yoked to and give some examples of people with whom we have a choice about being yoked to or not.

3. How does Rehoboam's decision affect our view of the elders in our congregation in light of 1 Peter 5:1-3? Should his story compel us to listen more carefully to the wisdom and teaching of these men?

4. How can we understand what the will of the Lord is, as is spoken of in Ephesians 5:17?

Chapter 7 — *Yours* Completely

King Jeroboam — Having a Heart that is Fully Devoted to God means:
Having a Heart that is God-Serving

2 Minute Decompress — Breath slowly in and out three times. Read the entirety of Psalm 63.

> "O God, You are my God; I shall seek you earnestly;
> My soul thirsts for You, my flesh yearns for You,
> In a dry and weary land where there is no water."
> (vs. 1)

From Ponder to Pen — Take a moment to answer this question — Why do you serve God?

King Jeroboam's story is found in:
1 Kings 12:16-13:34 and 2 Chronicles 10:12-13:22

For this chapter we are going to do something a little different: a little thing I like to call "Pick it Apart". Sounds like fun, doesn't it? In "Pick it Apart" we are going to take an in-depth look at 1 Kings 12:25-13:34 and pick apart the information that is given there. We need to understand how to have a heart that is God-serving, as opposed to a heart that is self-serving. King Jeroboam is going to provide us with one of our examples of what *not* to do if we want to be completely devoted to God.

Chapter 7 – Having a Heart that is Serving God

Part One

READ 1 KINGS 12:25-27

In this passage we can see that Jeroboam was worried. He thought that when the people went to Jerusalem to sacrifice that they would leave serving him (in the kingdom of Israel) and go back to the house of David (in the kingdom of Judah), where Rehoboam was reigning as king at that time. Does Jeroboam know *for a fact* that the people would return to the house of David?

Instead of trusting in God (not something that the kings of Israel would be known for), Jeroboam borrowed trouble. Jeroboam was worried that if he didn't give the people of Israel a reason to stay, they would kill him, return to Judah and serve King Rehoboam instead of him. He decided he was going to do something to prevent their desertion from happening. How often do we jump right in to prevent something that we *think* will happen, when we really ought to simply just put our trust in God? Can you think of any examples in your life when you have done this?

READ 1 KINGS 12:28-32

Jeroboam devised a solution to his problem. In this solution he shows us that his heart was not fully devoted to God and that he was a king who was self-serving when he should have a been a king that was God-serving. Essentially, Jeroboam was a control freak. As someone who struggles with being a bit of a control-freak myself, I understand the struggle. But, there are times when our desire for control can get out of hand. Control has a lot to do with self. When our desire for control keeps us from trusting our spouse, co-workers, friends, church family or God, we often end up sinning or at the very least we find ourselves in a difficult situation because we have lost the ability to trust. When our desire for control keeps us from doing God's will, then it has become a serious spiritual problem!

King Jeroboam wanted so much to be the man in charge that he disregarded the commands of the Lord regarding worship and instituted things that he had devised in his own heart (1 Kings 12:33).

- Instead of leading the people to worship God, he made two golden calves for them to worship.
- Instead of allowing them to fulfill God's commandment to worship in Jerusalem, he moved their location of worship to Bethel and Dan where he had placed the golden calves. And he made houses on high places as well.
- He made priests from among people who were not Levites and were not to be called priests.
- He set his own feasts on days of his own choosing according to his own will and desire.

We can see from these verses that instead of obeying the things that God had authorized and instructed His people to do, King Jeroboam made his own plan for worship. He changed God's plan for worshipping Him to make it easier (essentially more pleasing) for the people. Don't we see the same thing happening today? This isn't a new problem. In the Christian Age today, worship is still being altered and changed from God's plan. Men authorize for themselves worship practices that are not heard of or practiced in the New Testament. And many times it is under the guise of "God never said not to".

God never said *not* to worship in Bethel or Dan. God never said *not* to institute new and different feast days. But, He didn't have to, did He? All He had to do (and did) was give instructions for worship to be made in Jerusalem. By that command He made it clear that no other place was according to His will. All He had to do (and did) was to command what religious feasts were to be held on what days and it was clear that no other man-made religious feast on no other day would be acceptable to Him. God made it clear what His people were to do. Yet, Jeroboam took it upon himself to practice things that had no part in God's plan and because of that he led Israel to sin.

FROM MOSES TO JEROBOAM TO YOU AND ME

Doing anything other than what God has said to do is exactly the sin that kept Moses from the Promised Land. Striking the rock wasn't just "doing things another way" in God's eyes, even though God had instructed it and accepted it before! For Moses, striking the rock was doing something other than what God had said to do. It was failing to treat Him as Holy (Numbers 20:12). For Jeroboam, devising his own way of worship was doing something other than what God had said to do. It was committing great sin (1 Kings 13:34). Today, God has made it clear in the New Testament how we are to worship Him. He has made clear the five acts of worship that the New Testament church engaged in on the first day of the week: heartfelt praying, sound Bible preaching, a capella singing, cheerful and generous giving, and reverent partaking of the Lord's supper. If we want to treat God as Holy, if we want to keep the Lord's church from great sin, then we should be careful not to do something other than what God has said to do. If we hold to the pattern (2 Timothy 1:13) laid out in the New Testament then we can rest assured we are serving God instead of serving ourselves.

I have no doubt that Jeroboam's self-serving choices were a result of his fears. He was afraid of what would happen to his position as king in the future if the people left Israel to worship in Jerusalem. As human beings, we understand what it is like to have fears when faced with change and an uncertain future. Maybe our numbers at church are shrinking. Maybe other churches in our town are growing by leaps and bounds. Maybe our singing is lacking spiritual uplift and needs revival. Those may be true! But, that doesn't mean it is time to find a new way to worship that is not found in the pages of the New Testament. That is the time for us to trust that God's way is the best way. That is the time to find revival within our hearts and according to the Word of God! If God's Word holds the answers to our worldly problems, doesn't it stand to reason that even more so God would give us the answers to the spiritual problems we face as the body of Christ? Most resoundingly – YES!

A Closer Look at Verses 30-31...

In verse 30 we see that a major problem arose because of Jeroboam's decision. "Now this thing became a sin for the people..." This sin would become such a large problem and a turning point for the people of Israel that throughout the rest of the reign of the kings of Israel over and over we read the words, "He did evil in the sight of the Lord and walked in the way of Jeroboam the son of Nebat, who caused Israel to sin".

In verse 31 we see yet another major problem. King Jeroboam called men priests who were not from the tribe of Levi. He did something similar to calling a monkey a "fish". No matter how often you call a monkey a "fish" it does not make it a fish. There is nothing about its hairy body, long tail, yowling call or big smile that makes it a fish. You can call a monkey a fish all day long, but it's still a monkey. Are we guilty of the same offense? Not calling a monkey a fish, but calling people "priests" who are not priests? The New Testament gives us clear commands to follow in order to become a Christian, to be added to the royal priesthood of God (1 Peter 2:9). Just as we see those in the New Testament doing in order to become Christians, we also must hear God's word (Romans 10:17), believe it with all our hearts (Acts 4:4), repent of our sins (Acts 17:30-31), confess Christ as the Son of God (1 John 4:15) and be baptized for the forgiveness of our sins (Acts 2:37-38). We cannot be a Christian by any other way. Yet, how often do we hear people called "Christians" simply because they claim to follow Christ or have Christ-like qualities? Many people claim to be a Christian because they asked Jesus in to their hearts as their personal Lord and Savior. Many claim to be Christians because they believe in God and try to be good people. But, what is troubling is that those descriptions are not found anywhere in the New Testament and can in no way make them a Christian, a member of the royal priesthood of God. Are we guilty of calling people "Priests" who are not priests just as Jeroboam did? Just some food for thought...

Part 2

READ 1 KINGS 13:1-10

While these verses seemingly have nothing to do with King Jeroboam, they become the lead-in for the next part of the story. This section of the story is about a man of God who came to deliver a message from God against King Jeroboam and the priests who were following him. He said that human bones would be burned on the altar in Bethel (which would come true in the time of King Josiah in 2 Kings 23:15-18). This prophesy infuriated Jeroboam and he commanded the man of God to be seized. However, as Jeroboam reached out to give the command, his hand dried up and he could not pull it back to himself. What a freaky thing to happen I am sure! Jeroboam seemed to be instantly humbled at that point, but like seed falling on shallow ground, it came up quickly and died. He begged the man of God to heal his hand and God granted his request, but Jeroboam soon forgot God's mercy on him and returned to his self-serving ways.

Following this, King Jeroboam said he wanted to honor the man of God (or maybe get in his good graces?). He invited him to his home to refresh himself. However, the man of God refused Jeroboam's invitation on the reasoning that he must follow God's command to eat or drink nothing and to return home by a different way.

Now, bear with me, because at first glance there doesn't seem to be a connection between Part 1 – Jeroboam's sin and Part 2 and 3 – The story of the man of God. But, there is! I promise!

Part 3

READ 1 KINGS 13:11-17

There was an old prophet living in Bethel (one of the places where Jeroboam had put a golden calf for worship) who heard about the man of God and what had been done regarding Jeroboam. So, this old prophet went to the man of God and invited him to come home and eat with him. The man of God told the old prophet no, just as God had commanded him to do. Now remember, that not all prophets are from God. King Rehoboam had 400 prophets and they all blatantly lied to him about the outcome of the battle of Ramoth-Gilead. A prophet is simply someone who claims to make predictions about the future. In the Old Testament we see many people making

Chapter 7 – Having a Heart that is Serving God

claims about future events, but God always reveals the truth or the falsehood of their words in His good time.

READ 1 KINGS 13:18-19

"He said to him, 'I am also a prophet like you, and and angel spoke to me by the word of the Lord, saying, "Bring him back with you to your house, that he may eat bread and drink water."' But he lied to him. So he went back with him, and ate bread in his house and drank water."

We do not know for sure why the old prophet tried to persuade the man of God to go against what God had told him to do. Maybe to teach the Israelites a lesson. Maybe to teach us a lesson! The reality is that a red flag should have gone up in the mind of the man of God when the word of the Lord changed! The man of God should have stopped to ask of God if this was His will instead of just following blindly. Just because the old prophet claimed to have a new message from an angel of the Lord was no reason to accept it as true. Sure, he was hungry and thirsty from his traveling. Who wouldn't be? But, he had been given a specific command to follow. He was given a task to be God-serving, but he ended up being self-serving instead.

READ 1 KINGS 13:20-25

As a result of his self-serving actions, punishment comes to the man of God. After he left the house of the old prophet, he was killed by a lion on the road. At first, it might seem like an abrupt ending to a pointless story, but this account is far from pointless. Can you tell yet how these three stories connect? Like three acts in a play, the lesson to be learned isn't obvious until the end.

Jeroboam acted without consulting God. He did was what pleasing to himself (self-serving) instead of what was pleasing to God (God-serving). The man of God did the very same thing. Sure, we feel sorry for him because he was lied to, but the word of the Lord had come to him directly and he traded it out for the *alleged* word of an angel who had *supposedly* spoken to a man (the old prophet) whom he didn't even know before that day. That's as bad as believing the story about your best friend's neighbor's cousin's co-worker who won a new car by playing "rock, paper, scissors". Did it really happen? Possibly. But, how can you know for sure? Only by going to the source. Could the old prophet have been telling the man of God the truth? Possibly. But, how could he know for sure? Only by going to the source. He could have consulted the Lord, but he chose to feed his physical hunger over seeking God's will and he paid a very dear price.

It is the same for us today. When faced with an unfamiliar religious teaching we have to "go to the source" – God's Word.

Would Jeroboam learn his lesson?

The old prophet was from Bethel, the territory of King Jeroboam. Word would very likely have gotten back to King Jeroboam about what became of the man of God who pronounced a curse on his altar at Bethel. King Jeroboam was offered an opportunity to learn a valuable and life-changing lesson that could have turned him from his self-serving ways. He could have seen the great cost of not serving God and not consulting His will (or His Law) before acting. But, Jeroboam did not turn from his evil way. He continued on the road that he desired to be on. It is a pity for those who do not care about God's will because they do not know God's will (and it is our job to teach them!). But woe to those, like Jeroboam, who know God's will and still do not care! King Jeroboam just didn't care about serving

God. He only cared about serving his own desires and doing things the way he wanted to do them.

And what was the result? In 1 Kings 15:25-30 his son, Nadab, became king. Nadab did evil and continued in the footsteps of his father. Evil continued to reign in the house of Israel because Jeroboam introduced it and Nadab continued it. It wasn't long until a man named Baasha from the tribe of Issachar came along. He killed Nadab and became the new king. Then, in a dramatic and pitiful ending to a dynasty that had every opportunity to serve God, Baasha proceeded to kill the entire house of Jeroboam just as it was prophesied in 1 Kings 13:34.

WILL WE LEARN FROM JEROBOAM'S LESSON?

King Jeroboam's life teaches us that a self-serving way of life that continues un-checked will *always* bring about the ruin of godly people and their children. We must take care to devote ourselves to God by being God-serving in every aspect of our lives – in our conduct, in our worship, in our homes and workplaces. It is not about what we want or what we like that is important. Those things are secondary to serving our God.

My challenge to you is for you to pinpoint that one thing (among the many?) that you battle most in your effort to be His Completely. We all have our struggles. I, Cindy Baker, am self-serving when I do everything in my home, except sit down to study my Bible and pray. I may have the dishes washed, the house picked up, the laundry done, flowers planted, kids entertained, and even a little time for a rest, or to watch something on Netflix. But, if I haven't taken the time to stop and spend some time with God, then I am self-serving, not God-serving. I am telling you this from personal experience because it is something I battle every single day! Like I said, we all have our struggles. However, we must strive to overcome them so we can be fully devoted, His completely.

Chapter 7 – Having a Heart that is Serving God

QUESTIONS FOR FURTHER STUDY

1. In what area of your life do you have trouble giving up control and trusting others or trusting God?

2. Why is it so hard for people to give up worshipping God with instruments?

3. Is *a capella* singing in worship simply a "tradition of men" that we follow or does it have Biblical basis? How does Scripture support your argument? How does history support your argument?

4. Comparing Mark 7:9 and 2 Thessalonians 2:15, when is following tradition wrong and when is it right?

5. What changes do you need to make in your daily life to be God-serving instead of self-serving?

CHAPTER 8 — *Yours* COMPLETELY

King Jehoshaphat — HAVING A HEART THAT IS FULLY DEVOTED TO GOD MEANS:
Taking Pride in the Ways of God

2 Minute Decompress – Breath slowly in and out three times. In 2 Chronicles 20:20 King Jehoshaphat makes a two-sentence statement to the people of Israel that packs a powerful punch.

> "They rose early in the morning and went out to the wilderness of Tekoa; and when they went out, Jehoshaphat stood and said, **'Listen to me, O Judah and inhabitants of Jerusalem, put your trust in the Lord your God and you will be established. Put your trust in His prophets and succeed.'"**

From Ponder to Pen – If King Jehoshaphat were speaking to us today I can just imagine him saying, "Listen to me, you followers of Jesus Christ, put your trust in the Lord your God and you will be established. Put your trust in His Word and succeed." Consider, what does Jehoshaphat's plea to God's People in 2 Chronicles 20:20 mean for your life today?

KING JEHOSHAPHAT'S STORY IS FOUND IN:
1 Kings 15:23-24; 22:1-50 and 2 Chronicles chapters 17-20

History reveals Jehoshaphat to be one of the good kings of Israel. And it is no wonder why. He had his failings (he never did get those

Chapter 8 – Taking Pride in the ways of God

high places removed once and for all) and his foolish decisions – "Sure, Evil King Ahaziah, I'll help you build some boats," (an undertaking that literally went flat - 2 Chronicles 20:37). Despite those things, King Jehoshaphat was a man who strove to lead the people of Judah to follow God. What set him apart from the rest of the kings was that Jehoshaphat was a man who "took great pride in the ways of the Lord" (2 Chronicles 17:6).

With so many valuable nuggets of wisdom to take from the life of King Jehoshaphat, I am hard put as a writer to narrow it down enough to keep this chapter from going on and on and on! So, we'll just focus on the main lessons we can learn from him. And they are good ones!

What does it mean to take pride in something? The dictionary describes pride as "a person or thing that is the object or source of a feeling of deep pleasure or satisfaction". For God to note King Jehoshaphat as a man who "took pride in the ways of the Lord" shows how deeply Jehoshaphat loved His God. Once again we see that having a heart that is fully devoted to God means that there is a perfect harmony of our emotional love for God and our every day actions of obedience. Taking pride in the ways of the Lord is love in action at its best!

How did Jehoshaphat take Pride in the Ways of the Lord?

2 Chronicles 17:3-9 sums it up for us. These verses hit all the high points of his fully devoted heart.

1. **He realized the power of example** (verse 3).

Once again, we see David used as the measuring stick for loyalty to God. Jehoshephat was noted to follow in the early footsteps of David when David was called by Samuel to be a man after God's own heart. David's early life was one of courage in the face of trials and reliance on God. These are attributes we see in Jehoshaphat's life as he put political peace on the line in order to seek God's leading and also in his prayer to God when he was faced with impending doom.

Let's look at 2 Chronicles 20:1-20. At this time King Jehoshaphat receives word that a "great multitude" of the sons of Moab, sons of Ammon and some of the Meunites had come to make war on Judah. King Jehoshaphat is naturally filled with fear as anyone might be when on the brink of being attacked.

What was his reaction? He could have chosen to lead the people in attack immediately. He could have chosen to cower in fear, wring his hands and worry himself sick. But, he didn't choose any of those things. He chose to rely on God. It wasn't passive, - "Well, since I don't know what else to do I guess I'll ask God to help." Verse 3 says that "Jehoshaphat was afraid and turned his attention to seek the Lord...".

He was in command of his emotions. He knew what he had to do and where his attention should lie. He could have turned his attention to all the obstacles before him. He could have turned his attention to other gods. But, he didn't. He turned his attention to the Lord and sought God's leading.

What makes Jehoshaphat so great is that he didn't just do it for himself, but he led the people of Judah to do the same. He knew the value of leading by example. In his life he followed the example of King David and he also followed the example set by his father, Asa.

Chapter 8 – Taking Pride in the ways of God

He took those lessons he learned and he led the people by his own example.

Next, King Jehoshaphat proclaimed a fast throughout all Judah and led the people to seek their help from the Lord. I absolutely love verses 5-12. They are words that hold great power and show us Jehoshaphat's devotion to God and how he took absolute pride in the ways of God. It's a bit of a long passage, but worth it to read and ponder!

> *"Then Jehoshaphat stood in the assembly of Judah and Jerusalem, in the house of the LORD before the new court, and he said, 'O LORD, the God of our fathers, are You not God in the heavens? And are You not ruler over all the kingdoms of the nations? Power and might are in Your hand so that no one can stand against You. Did You not, O our God, drive out the inhabitants of this land before Your people Israel and give it to the descendants of Abraham Your friend forever? They have lived in it, and have built You a sanctuary there for Your name, saying "Should evil come upon us, the sword, or judgment, or pestilence, or famine, we will stand before this house and before You (for Your name is in this house) and cry to You in our distress, and You will hear and deliver us." Now behold, the sons of Ammon and Moab and Mount Seir, whom You did not let Israel invade when they came out of the land of Egypt (they turned aside from them and did not destroy them), see how they are rewarding us by coming to drive us out from Your possession which You have given us as an inheritance. O our God, will You not judge them? For we are powerless before this great multitude who are coming against us; nor do we know what to do, but our eyes are on You.'"*

How many times do we find ourselves agonizing over a problem? How many times are we afraid, lonely, heartbroken, faced with an overwhelming decision, or a problem that seems too difficult for us to work through? It is at these times that we should fall to our knees in prayer and follow the example of Jehoshaphat saying, "O my God, I do not know what to do, but my eyes are on You". That, my friends, is what it means to be His Completely.

2. **He set his heart to seek God** (verse 4).

Point One kind of runs into Point Two at this junction because we see how King Jehoshaphat sought God in times of trouble, ready and wanting to rely on Him.

We can also see how he sought God's direction when faced with a decision to make. In 2 Chronicles chapter 18, King Ahab of Israel came to Jehoshaphat seeking his help in going up against Ramoth-Gilead. Being the peacemaker that he was, Jehoshaphat readily agreed and then kind of backtracked a step or two and insisted that they inquire for the word of the Lord first before doing anything. Ahab, not being one to follow God, decided that his own men (400 of them) and his own prophets could supply the needed information to his question in verse 5, "Shall we go against Ramoth-gilead to battle, or shall I refrain?"

King Ahab's prophets had nothing but good things to say about how this battle would turn out, filling his ears and fueling his hopes of "goring the Arameans until they are consumed". But, this isn't good enough for Jehoshaphat. He knows that a prophet of a king may be exalted by men, but is not the same thing as a prophet who has been chosen by God. Jehoshaphat may be a peacemaker, but in verse 6 he shows that he is also willing to risk his political relationship in order to follow God's leading. "But Jehoshaphat said, 'Is there not yet a prophet of the Lord here that we may inquire of him?'" The Lord's prophet Micaiah does not give the message that King Ahab wants to hear. In verse 16 he prophesied that at the end of the battle Israel will be as "sheep without a shepherd" because King Ahab would not live through the battle in order to lead them.

In the end, King Jehoshaphat went with King Ahab into battle and lived to tell about it, but King Ahab met his end, just as God's prophet had said.

It wasn't long after this occurrence that Jehu, who was the son of Hanani the seer (a seer is someone who is said to be able to see what the future holds) came and basically called Jehoshaphat on the carpet for his alliance with King Ahab, a known man of wickedness. Jehu's assessment of King Jehoshaphat's foolish decision that nearly cost him his life shows us that Jehoshaphat was a man who was just like you and me. He was a follower of God who tried to do the right thing, but sometimes failed and made poor choices. Overall, though, Jehu realized that King Jehoshaphat was trying to do the right thing and gave him a great commendation when he said, "You have set your heart to seek God" (2 Chronicles 19:3).

3. **He followed God's commandments** (verse 4).

We don't have every detail of the ways Jehoshaphat followed God's commands, but he is given recognition in the Scriptures for keeping Judah from worshipping the Baals (something that King Ahab of Israel failed to do). He succeeded in removing the Asherim/Ashteroth idols from the land (2 Chronicles 17:6, 19:3). However, it seems that he struggled with allowing worship on the high places. First he removed them (17:6). Then, at some point he allowed them to be brought back (20:33).

Jehoshaphat also upheld a high standard for the judges that he appointed. 2 Chronicles 19:5-11 reveals that not only did he take personal pride in the ways of God, but he also held others to this standard. When he appointed judges in the land, he commissioned them to carry out their work according to the Law of the Lord. On top of that, he urged them to give their best. "He said to the judges, 'Consider what you are doing, for you do not judge for man but for the Lord who is with you when you render judgment'" (2 Chronicles 19:6).

I find it interesting that this commission of Jehoshaphat's is carried over to the New Testament and is given by Paul in Colossians 3:17, "Whatever you do in word or deed, do all in the name of the Lord Jesus, giving thanks through Him to God the Father." Many people read this verse to mean that it doesn't matter what you do so long as you proclaim it to be in the name of the Lord Jesus. However, the phrase "in the name of" in this verse literally means "by the authority of". Because of its Greek meaning, we know that the things that we do must be in accordance with God's will. Verse 23 goes on to say that "Whatever you do, do your work heartily, as for the Lord rather than for men". For us, as Christians, that is what it means to take pride in the things we do.

In what aspects of your life do you need to remember that you are not just working for men, but for God?

Chapter 8 – Taking Pride in the ways of God

4. **He set himself apart from those who were not following God** (verse 4).

   Sometimes it is hard to be different. But, as God's people, we are called to talk, act, and think in a different way than those in the world. King Jehoshaphat recognized this and as verse four says, he "did not act as Israel did". We have already noted that between the two kingdoms, Israel was by far more corrupt. They were led by wicked leaders who had no thought of following God and thus led the people to do the same. However, Jehoshaphat showed himself to be different. He was set apart. He sought after God and followed His commands as the beginning part of verse four reads.

   1 Corinthians 6:9-10 is a laundry list of sins that the members of the church in Corinth had been guilty of in the past, things that had the power to keep them from inheriting the kingdom of God. However, in verse 11 the apostle Paul makes a distinction that something happened to change the hearts and lives of those people. They were once sinners and then they were saved. They were once just like everyone else and then they were set apart for something greater! "Such were some of you; but you were washed, but you were sanctified, but you were justified in the name of the Lord Jesus Christ and in the Spirit of our God." We have been called to be set apart from the rest of the world. That means that we need to talk, act and think in a different way than those around us who are not Christians. Why? Because we, too, have been washed, sanctified, and justified through Christ and the Spirit of our God!

   Name some specific ways you can show those in your workplace, school, neighborhood or community that you are different from those who do not follow God.

5. **He made reading God's Word a priority** (verses 7-9).

   Extra points to anyone who can read verses 7 and 8 three times fast! What a tongue-twisting list of people! No matter how hard it is to pronounce all those names, what they did was a great thing! "They taught in Judah, having the book of the law of the Lord with them; and they went throughout all the cities of Judah and taught among the people" (verse 9).

   King Jehoshaphat set himself apart from the kings of Israel because he believed in the Word of God. He took pride in the ways of God and he was going to ensure that the rest of Judah would take pride in those ways as well. He knew that there was only one way to make that happen and that was to teach the people the law of the Lord. So, he sent the officials and priests to get it done.

   There is no other way to say it – we must make reading God's Word a priority in our lives! Take it in – every day! Read and ponder a scripture of the day, participate in every opportunity you have for in-depth Bible Study, read with your family and talk about the Scriptures. There are countless ways to accomplish this task! We must spend time in God's Word if we expect to grow as Christians. I marvel at the number of times I hear of people who claim to have been a Christian for years, but really know very little about the Bible beyond the classic Sunday School Bible stories.

   If we claim to follow Christ, we must crack that spine (or open the App!) and learn more about His Word. How can we take pride in the ways of God if we are never in the Word reading about His ways? It is not just something that we do as our "Christian duty", but God wants us to hunger and thirst for the righteousness that comes through His Word. The funny thing about Bible reading is the more you read the more you *want* to read! Maybe it is not so

Chapter 8 – Taking Pride in the ways of God

funny after all; God's Word has power! God knows that the inner depths and yearnings of our soul can only be fed by the Bread of Life, which is His Word. Without it, we will spiritually starve and die. And with it we will grow stronger and feast upon the abundant life that Christ is offering to us.

So, open up the Word and let King Jehoshaphat's example lead you to take pride in the ways of God.

QUESTIONS FOR FURTHER STUDY

1. What are some things in your life that you take pride in? How can you use those things to bring glory to God?

2. Is there anything in your life that you need to let go of and just pray, "O my God, I do not know what to do, but my eyes are on You"? What would it be?

3. Have you ever had to pray that prayer about a situation in the past? How did you feel when you finally made the decision to trust in God?

4. What does it mean to live our Christian lives (i.e. conduct, choices, worship) by God's authority according to Colossians 3:17?

Chapter 9 – Acquiring Spiritual Clarity

CHAPTER 9 — *Yours* COMPLETELY

King Ahab — HAVING A HEART THAT IS FULLY DEVOTED TO GOD MEANS:
Acquiring Spiritual Clarity

2 Minute Decompress — Breath slowly in and out three times. Read Psalm 36:1-4.

> "Transgression speaks to the ungodly within his heart;
> There is no fear of God before His eyes.
> For it flatters him in his own eyes
> Concerning the discovery of his iniquity and the hatred of it.
> The words of his mouth are wickedness and deceit;
> He has ceased to be wise and to do good;
> He does not despise evil."

From Ponder to Pen — The words of Psalm 36 are words worth contemplating. In contrast to verses 1-4, verses 5-9 go on to describe the joy of living a godly life. Verse 9 reads, "For with You is the fountain of life; In Your light we see light."

It is difficult to clearly see light, to appreciate the blessings of being in Christ, when our vision is clouded by the sin in our life. Why is that?

KING AHAB'S STORY IS FOUND IN:
1 Kings 16:29 through 22:40; and 2 Chronicles 18:1-34

Chapter 9 – Acquiring Spiritual Clarity

SEEING OUR SIN AS TRIVIAL

It is easy to look at others and see the gravity of their sin, but when it comes to our own, we tend to trivialize our sin. How often do we tell ourselves it is just a day at the pool when we are really drowning in our iniquity? We let ourselves think that our sin is small, insignificant, no big deal… not like _____'s sin! Deep down inside, we know what we are doing when we make excuses and try to justify our sin. As difficult as it is to change our perception, we must change it! We must see our sin the way God sees it. Only then will we acquire spiritual clarity.

> What are some examples of things that we tend to trivialize and convince ourselves that they have little impact on our spiritual clarity?
>
> Is there a sin you struggle with that you find yourself trying to justify?

Have you ever had "Scarlett O'Hara Syndrome"? Most of us have read *Gone with the Wind* by Maragret Mitchell (1936) or watched the movie based on the book. For all her short-comings, one thing I love about Scarlett is her determination not to dwell on things. She often says, "I won't think of it now. I'll think of it tomorrow." In some instances that kind of mindset is good. After all, today has enough trouble of its own (Matthew 6:34). However, when it comes to our sin, Scarlett's attitude is not the one to take! We must not convince ourselves that we can live it up today and let it go until tomorrow. In truth, when it comes to our sin, we should *give it up* today, so we can start anew tomorrow with hearts that are fully devoted to God.

KING AHAB MAKES HIS MARK

1 Kings 16:31-33 is a laundry list of King Ahab's sins. Let's look at what they were:

- He saw it as a trivial thing to walk in the sins of Jeroboam.
- He led Israel to do the same, walking in the sins of Jeroboam.
- He foolishly married Jezebel.
    - She was a wicked woman (shown by her actions in 1 Kings 19 and 21).
    - She was a Baal worshipper.
- He left God's commands to serve Baal and worship him.
- He erected an altar to Baal in Samaria, the capital of the Northern Kingdom of Israel.
- He made yet another idol, the Asherah (a wooden symbol of female deity).
- He provoked God more than all the other kings of Israel before him.

And then, of course, we can also add these to the list as his story unfolds:

- He relentlessly tormented God's prophet, Elijah (18:17, 19:10).
- He neglected to do God's will with Ben-Hadad (20:34, 42).
- He was greedy and knowingly condescended to the murder of Naboth, just to gain a vineyard (21:13).
- He sold himself to do evil in the sight of the Lord (21:20).
- He tried to hide from God by disguising himself in battle (22:30).

In this chapter we are going to look at how we can have spiritual clarity and we are going to use the example of King Ahab to do it – not because he did things so right, but because he did things so wrong! He was a king who is another example of what *not* to do if you want to have a heart that is fully devoted to God. Good 'ol Ahab, he just provides us with so many examples for learning! He probably had no idea that his spiritual blindness would be so useful for our spiritual clarity.

SEEING SIN THE WAY GOD SEES IT

Let's look at 1 Kings 17:1 as it sets the scene for the story of Elijah and the prophets of Baal. In this verse God's prophet, Elijah, predicted that there would be famine in the land for three years. If we go on to read 1 Kings 18:2 it says that the famine was severe in Samaria. Normally, when there is adversity in people's lives, they turn to the Lord for help. This is just the way of man. However, King Ahab was an obstinate man, determined to be devoted to himself and his evil wife instead of being devoted to God. In this time of famine he did not turn to the Lord and he continued to lead Israel to worship the Baals.

As a prophet of God, it was Elijah's work to turn the hearts of the people back to God. And did he ever have his work cut out for him with King Ahab! Ahab wanted nothing to do with God and nothing to do with God's prophet. He didn't just shun Elijah; he set himself to make Elijah's life as difficult as possible. In 1 Kings 18:17-18 Ahab calls Elijah "You troubler of Israel". Troublemakers rarely have a clear view of themselves and the strife they create. True to form, Ahab is quick to call Elijah a troublemaker (simply for doing the work of the Lord). Elijah wants to turn the hearts of the people. Ahab wants the people to stay exactly where they are. No wonder he chaffed under Elijah's efforts!

How does Elijah respond to King Ahab's accusation? In verse 18 Elijah responds, (and I can just hear the consternation in his voice!) "I have not troubled Israel, but you and your father's house have, because you have forsaken the commandments of the Lord and you have followed the Baals." Whatcha gonna say to that Ahab? He cannot deny this truth. He knows that he does not follow God and he made the conscious decision to lead Israel to worship the Baals. The problem wasn't just that Ahab did those things, but that he didn't see it as any big deal to "walk in the ways of Jeroboam". King Jeroboam was self-serving and did not consult God's will before he led Israel into sin by devising his own ways of worship and his own feast days. King Ahab walked the same path. Oh, the scenery was different, but the road still led to the same place – farther away from God.

GOD ISSUES A CHALLENGE

On Mount Carmel, in 1 Kings 18:20-46, the prophet Elijah calls the people to make a decision. Evidently some were waffling back and forth. You can almost hear them muttering to themselves, "Should we follow God? Should we follow Ahab? Yes, God gave us His commands, but that was a long time ago and Ahab is our king and he is here now. See how powerful he is?" God has had enough and His prophet Elijah calls on the people to make a decision in verse 21. "How long will you hesitate between two opinions? If the Lord is God, follow Him; but if Baal, follow him." This passage shows us that we can't live on both sides of the fence. God owns His side and Satan owns his, but Satan also owns the fence! We must choose to be fully devoted to God or we will find ourselves devoted to the enemy of God. We can't have it both ways or try to live a little on both sides. Just like the song asks, "Tell me whose side are you livin' on"?

In 1 Kings 18:19-24 Elijah sets the rules for God's challenge. Notice that the people of Israel, the 450 prophets of Baal and the 400 prophets of Asherah were not forced into anything. They all agreed

Chapter 9 – Acquiring Spiritual Clarity

to Elijah's (God's) suggestion, proclaiming it to be a good idea. Here's what the challenge would look like:

- Each side would get an ox and cut it up.
- Each side would place it on wood with no fire under it.
- Each side would call to his god/ or God.
- The God who answered by fire would be proclaimed, "He is God".

All day long – morning until night – the worshippers of Baal called to him to bring fire to their sacrifice. They cried in loud voices and leapt around the altar. The more I read about Elijah, the more I like him! After the people had been calling to Baal for half the day with no reply, Elijah gets a little sarcastic with them. "It came about at noon, that Elijah mocked them and said, 'Call out with a loud voice, for he is a god; either he is occupied or gone aside or is on a journey, or perhaps he is asleep and needs to be awakened'" (verse 27). But, the prophets of Baal fail to see his sarcasm. So, what do the worshippers of Baal do? They cry louder and take their antics up a notch, cutting themselves with swords and lances. They take such extreme measures to get their god's attention! Aren't you grateful that our God does not require these extreme measures when we call on Him? For all the effort they made, did it help them? Not in the least! By evening, after a full day's efforts, verse 29 says, "But there was no voice, no one answered, and no one paid attention".

Then, Elijah takes it to the next level with his sacrifice to God. He is going to show them once and for all how His God is all powerful, able to do above and beyond what the prophets of Baal thought their god would be able to do.

- He repaired the altar of the Lord that had been torn down.

- He used 12 stones according to the number of the sons of Jacob.
- He made a trench around the altar.
- He put on the wood and the ox that was cut in pieces.
- Then he instructed for 12 pitchers of water to be poured over the sacrifice until it filled the trench. This action would put the prophets of Baal to shame, as their god could not even light a *dry* sacrifice!

Then Elijah called to God in verses 36-37 to "let it be known that You are God in Israel and that I am Your servant and I have done all these things at Your word. Answer me, O Lord, answer me, that this people may know that You, O Lord, are God, and that You have turned their heart back again."

Not only did God answer by lighting the sacrifice on fire, but the fire of God fell on the offering consuming it *and* consuming the wood *and* the stones *and* all the water in the trench as well. What a show that must have been! So amazing was the response from The One, True Almighty God that "when all the people saw it, they fell on their faces; and they said, 'The Lord, He is God; the Lord, He is God.'" And this same God we serve today!

AFTER THE SMOKE CLEARS

Why all the hooplah? Was it just to prove that God was all-powerful? Yes, that was part of it. Mostly though, Elijah did all this to try to open the eyes of King Ahab. Ahab was spiritually blinded by his sin. He was looking at his marriage, his idol worship, and his wickedness through the smoky haze of complacency and carelessness. He thought nothing of marrying an evil woman. He thought nothing of worshipping Baal. He thought nothing about how his actions were

Chapter 9 – Acquiring Spiritual Clarity

leading Israel into sin. He saw his sin as trivial. God used Elijah to teach Ahab a lesson to help bring about his spiritual clarity.

King Ahab had a choice – the same choice that the people were called to make on Mount Carmel. Would he turn and devote himself to God or would he continue to see his sin as trivial? Ahab had his choice and he chose to trivialize his sin and continue to walk in it. This same choice is facing us today – will we devote ourselves to God or will we continue to see our sin as trivial? Things that are trivial have no long-term repercussions. They simply don't matter like the color of paint I choose for my bedroom, the kind of car I drive, or whether I choose to live in the city or in the country. These decisions are trivial... they essentially do not have any bearing on my spiritual life. But, there are other things I do that matter and they matter a great deal. Galatians 5:19-21 warns us of sins that are far more than trivial:

> *"Now the deeds of the flesh are evident, which are: immorality, impurity, sensuality, idolatry, sorcery, enmities, strife, jealousy, outbursts of anger, disputes, dissensions, factions, envying, drunkenness, carousing, and things like these, of which I forewarn you, just as I have forewarned you, that those who practice such things will not inherit the kingdom of God."*

These deeds or choices are not just trivial things that have no bearing on our spiritual lives. They have eternal consequences and should be viewed as such.

Looking at King Ahab's life we can see that like King Jeroboam, he faltered at the words in Galatians 6:3, "For if anyone thinks he is something when he is nothing, he deceives himself." Standing on Mount Carmel Ahab quickly found out that God is not mocked. He sowed wickedness and reaped humiliation.

But, we can be different! We do not have to fall to the same sins that held King Ahab within their grasp! If we sow Bible study, prayer, wisdom and love, we will reap spiritual clarity. For we see that Galatians 6:8 holds a promise of something better when we are fully and completely devoted to God. *"For the one who sows to his own flesh will from the flesh reap corruption, but the one who sows to the Spirit will from the Spirit reap eternal life."*

Chapter 9 – Acquiring Spiritual Clarity

QUESTIONS FOR FURTHER STUDY

1. What is the danger in trivializing our own sin, but magnifying the sins of others?

2. What are some examples of times when "Scarlett O'Hara Syndrome" is a benefit?

3. What are some ways we sow to the Spirit, according to Galatians 6:8?

4. Why do we sometimes falter in our faith like the Israelites or find ourselves tossed back and forth in our devotion to God?

CHAPTER 10 — *Yours* COMPLETELY

King Hezekiah — HAVING A HEART THAT IS FULLY DEVOTED TO GOD MEANS:
Having a Heart that Trusts in God's Grace

2 Minute Decompress — Breath slowly in and out three times. Read the words to the song, *"His Grace Reaches Me"*.

> "Deeper than the ocean and wider than the sea,
> is the grace of the Savior for sinners like me;
> Sent from the Father and it thrills my soul,
> Just to feel and to know
> that His blood makes me whole.
>
> "Higher than the mountains and brighter than the sun,
> It was offered at Calvary for everyone;
> Greatest of treasures and it's mine today,
> Though my sins were as scarlet,
> He has washed them away.
>
> "His grace reaches me. Yes, His grace reaches me.
> And 'twill last through eternity.
> Now I'm under His control and I'm happy in my soul,
> Just to know that His grace reaches me."

(Words and Music by Jewell M. Whitey Gleason, 1964)

From Ponder to Pen — Read through Psalm 136. The concept of "mercy", "grace", and "lovingkindness" is expressed 26 times in this psalm. During worship we sing the words of *"His Grace Reaches Me"* and yet,

Chapter 10 – Having a Heart that Trusts in God's Grace

often, when we look at our lives, all we can see are our failures and wonder if God will say of us, "Well done, good and faithful servant". Why is that? Why do we have such a difficult time trusting in the power of God's grace?

KING HEZEKIAH'S STORY IS FOUND IN:

2 Kings 16:19-20; 18:1–20:21 and in 2 Chronicles 29:1–32:33. In addition, King Hezekiah is written of by the prophet Isaiah in Isaiah chapters 36-39.

The account and events surrounding King Hezekiah cover a good deal of scripture, compared to some of the other kings of Judah. Hezekiah is commended in 2 Chronicles 29:2 as doing "right in the sight of the Lord, according to all that his father David had done". King David was the measuring stick and Hezekiah met the standard well by the way he lived. He was a man who was fully devoted to God and because of that he worked hard to lead the Israelites back to God. As great as this accomplishment was, we will see that like King David, King Hezekiah was not perfect. He sinned. He was weak and foolish at times, but he stands out among all the kings of Judah because of His trust in God. Through Hezekiah, we are able to learn valuable lessons about God's grace and mercy. While King Hezekiah wasn't sinless, he was blameless because he sought the Lord with a whole heart and tried hard to do what was right in the eyes of the Lord.

Part 1 - An Overview of Hezekiah's Life

LEADING STRONG RIGHT OUT OF THE GATE

In the first year of his reign, Hezekiah did two great things that set the people of Judah on the right track back to God. Not just in the first year, but in the first *month* of his reign, he set himself to restore temple worship. He wasted no time! King Hezekiah recognized the folly of their fathers in the past. "For our fathers have been unfaithful and have done evil in the sight of the Lord our God, and have forsaken Him and turned their faces away from the dwelling place of the Lord, and have turned their backs" (2 Chronicles 29:6). He realized that something must change so he charged the priests and the Levites with the work of preparing the temple for worship once again. King Hezekiah showed us that it is never too late to make a change! In verse 19 we read how the utensils that were once used for worship had been cast aside by King Ahaz during his reign. But, like picking up a Bible that has been collecting dust for days on end, they were cleaned, prepared and rededicated to God for use in serving Him.

In 2 Chronicles chapter 30 King Hezekiah follows his first strong action with another. As soon as the temple was ready for use, he set about to reinstitute the celebration of the Passover. For too long the people of Judah had failed to remember how God had led them out of Egypt. For too long they had neglected this command that was designed to help them stay faithful to their God.

What a poignant lesson for us as well! When we fail to recognize all that God has done for us, when we neglect worship, when we are not partaking of the Lord's Supper and remembering each week the sacrifice that Jesus made on our behalf – how easy it is to fall away from doing the things that are pleasing to God. God commands worship, communion, prayer and Bible study for a reason! Not because He is a God of "rules" who Lords over us with a strong arm, but He commands these things because He loves us. In His infinite wisdom He knows that weekly worship and communion, daily prayer and Bible study are the things that will bring about the peaceful fruit of righteousness that will lead us unwaveringly to heaven's gate!

King Hezekiah gives a plea for a renewal of service to God, and he shows the people what their loving God will do for them if they will seek to rededicate themselves to be His completely.

> "Now do not stiffen your neck like your fathers, but yield to the LORD and enter His sanctuary which He has consecrated forever, and serve the LORD your God, that His burning anger may turn away from you. For if you return to the LORD, your brothers and your sons will find compassion before those who led them captive and will return to this land. For the LORD your God is gracious and compassionate, and will not turn His face away from you if you return to Him" (2 Chronicles 30:8-9).

When we forsake God's commandments to follow our own path or to make things in our life (our work, friends, school, hobbies, etc.) as a god to us, serving those things and making them more important than Christ and His church, it gives God a burning anger towards us. He accepts no other god in our life but Him. But, He is a God who is gracious and compassionate and we will see the abundant love He has for us in our lives if return to Him, seeking first his kingdom and His righteousness. How great is His lovingkindness toward us!

His Grace, Our Response

In 2 Chronicles 31:1-19 we read about all the reforms that King Hezekiah made to get Judah back to the way they ought to be in their relationship with God. You can see great effort that was made by

Hezekiah, as their leader, and the work that the people did to be fully devoted to God once again. Hezekiah told the people that if they would return to God, He would bestow on them His perfect grace and compassion. When we have sinned and turn our hearts back to God, He is there waiting faithfully for us. He wants more than anything to give us His grace and show us the bounds of His compassion. 1 John 1:9 says, "If we confess our sins, He is faithful and righteous to forgive us our sins and to cleanse us from all unrighteousness."

Sometimes we find that hard to understand. After all, we live in a give-and-get world for the most part. If we work hard and live well, we get good things, materially speaking. If we are lazy and make bad choices, we do not get those things. Personally, it is hard for me to comprehend how I can fail in my efforts to be fully devoted to Him, and yet God can still give me something good. I see my failures and I know I don't deserve His forgiveness or the hope of heaven. But, God gives them to me. Not because I deserve them or because of who I am, but because of who *He* is! He loves me and all He asks is that I return that love, that I see His truth, and that I continue to try to walk in it.

For anyone who has reached up and out of the depths of their sin and sought God's forgiveness, the natural response is thanksgiving! In verses 5-8 the people begin to bring their tithes and place them in heaps. This time of offering was not something that lasted a few hours or even a few days. For four months God's people brought their offerings, heaping them up in vast abundance! When God showers His grace on us, and when we truly realize what a precious and undeserved gift it is, we have no other course to take. In thanksgiving, we want nothing more than to offer our lives that we may be used by Him.

Chapter 10 – Having a Heart that Trusts in God's Grace

Good, Right and True — Can this be said of you?

2 Chronicles 31:20-21 summarizes all that King Hezekiah did in his work for God. What made him such an exceptional king?

> "Thus Hezekiah did throughout all Judah; and he did what was good, right and true before the Lord his God. Every work which he began in the service of the house of God in law and in commandment, seeking his God, he did with all his heart and prospered."

These verses give us the answer of what it means to be fully devoted to God. Once again, we see in God's Word that in order to be His completely it requires both our heart and our obedience. When Hezekiah worked for God his work was done:

1. Within the bounds of God's law and commandments.
2. Seeking God's will and good pleasure.
3. With all of his heart.

In 2 Kings 18:7 we read that the Lord was with Hezekiah throughout his life and that in all things he prospered. Why? Why would God choose to bless King Hezekiah like He did? Backing up to verse 5-6 we read precisely why God poured out His blessings on Hezekiah.

> "He trusted in the Lord, the God of Israel; so that after him there was none like him among all the kings of Judah, nor among those who were before him. For he clung to the Lord; he did not depart from following Him, but kept His commandments, which the Lord had commanded Moses."

King Hezekiah was a great man who did great things all because he loved God with his whole heart and was fully devoted to Him.

Part 2- Hezekiah's Dealings with Assyria

NAUSEATING NATION

We are going to get comfortable in 2 Kings now in chapters 18 and 19 as we ponder the words in 18:7 "And he rebelled against the king of Assyria and did not serve him." This is such a short sentence and seemingly unimportant...unless you know something about Assyria.

Assyria was a nation located northeast of Judah. The capital was Ninevah (sound familiar?). Assyria had already carried away Israel into captivity and were now seeking to conquer the rest of God's chosen people in overtaking Judah. When we think of Assyria taking Israel into captivity we don't often think about what that means. For myself, I always imagined it to be forced labor or imprisonment. But, for the Assyrians, captivity had a much different definition. Halley's Bible Handbook has this to say about Assyria, a description that makes me cringe even as I type it!:

> "They practiced cruelty. They skinned their prisoners alive, or cut off their hands, feet, noses, ears or put out their eyes, or pulled out their tongues, and made mounds of humans skulls, all to inspire terror" (H.H. Halley, 1965).

No wonder Jonah did not want to go to Ninevah! They were an evil people who sought to break the spirits of their captives in the most cruel ways possible. Knowing this, brings to light the courage and faith in God that King Hezekiah displayed by rebelling against the evil Assyrian king, Sennacherib.

FALLING SHORT

Still, King Hezekiah was not perfect. He had a moments of weakness in his life and one of them was during the time that Sennacherib

Chapter 10 – Having a Heart that Trusts in God's Grace

began to apply pressure on Judah and imposed a forced tribute of money on Hezekiah. Sennacherib required him to pay 300 talents of silver and 30 talents of gold. In his weakness of faith in God, Hezekiah gave in to the demands of this evil king in order to spare further abuse to the people of Judah. What's worse is the means by which he paid this tribute. Hezekiah took the silver from the house of the Lord! Can you imagine? That would be like using our Sunday collection to pay forced honor to a Muslim leader of the extremist militant group, ISIS, and support their "ethnic cleansing"! What honor do we, as Christians, have to give to a heathen group that takes pleasure in the abuse and killing of innocent people? None whatsoever! Hezekiah allowed his fear of the Assyrians to lead him to foolishly pay this tribute.

> Something to humbly consider... What would you do in the face of those like the Assyrians or ISIS? Would you have the courage to stand and fight? Or would you seek to appease their need for power in hopes of saving your earthly life?

I believe King Hezekiah hoped that his monetary honor would appease the Assyrian king and get him off their back, so to speak, so they could continue serving God in peace. But, it didn't work out that way. Sennacherib would not be satisfied until he conquered and defeated the people of Judah in the same way it had been done to Israel.

In 2 Kings 18:17-35 Sennacherib's spokesman, Rabshekah, came to the people of Judah and tried to convince them to surrender. He began by insulting the Lord God and His people, hoping to bring about their doubt and a loss of faith in God. Then, he added more fuel to the fire and tried to tempt them with promises of a better land if they will surrender to Assyria. I believe his hope was that they would think, "Well, our God is not helping us, so we will go with this king who has better things to offer". But, that was not how the cookie crumbled. As they were commanded to do, the people did not answer Rabshekah, even when he suggested that their God was like the gods of the other lands and would be unable to deliver them from his hand (verse 35).

King Hezekiah had emotions as any other man, and the taunts by Rabshekah brought him great distress. He had faltered once in his faith and it brought him no relief from the Assyrians. Now in his time of helplessness and distress he turned to the Lord God to save them. He "clung to the Lord" and sought the help from God's prophet Isaiah. He offered a most heartfelt prayer to God confirming his faith in Him and pleading for God's deliverance.

> "Hezekiah prayed before the LORD and said, 'O LORD, the God of Israel, who are enthroned above the cherubim, You are the God, You alone, of all the kingdoms of the earth. You have made heaven and earth. Incline Your ear, O LORD, and hear; open Your eyes, O LORD, and see; and listen to the words of Sennacherib, which he has sent to reproach the living God. Truly, O LORD, the kings of Assyria have devastated the nations and their lands and have cast their gods into the fire, for they were not gods but the work of men's hands, wood and stone. So they have destroyed them. Now, O LORD our God, I pray, deliver us from his hand that all the kingdoms of the earth may know that You alone, O LORD, are God'" (2 Kings 19:15-19).

King Hezekiah must know that he does not deserve God's help and compassion, especially after he faltered in his foolish tribute to

Sennacherib. However, showing himself to be fully devoted to God, King Hezekiah trusted in God's grace.

GRACE EXTENDED

In 2 Kings 19:20-37 the prophet Isaiah gave a prophesy concerning King Hezekiah's plea for salvation from Assyria. God bestowed His grace on Judah because King Hezekiah sought him in a time of trouble with his whole heart, and the conclusion of Assyria's assault on Judah lies in verses 35-36. An angel of the Lord was sent and struck down 185,000 men in the camp of the Assyrians. As a result Sennacherib retreated back to Ninevah with his tail between his legs.

In 1815, Lord Byron wrote a poem called "The Destruction of Sennacherib". It begins with the majesty and power of the Assyrian nation...

> *"The Assyrian came down like the wolf on the fold,*
> *And his cohorts were gleaming in purple and gold;*
> *And the sheen of their spears was like stars on the sea,*
> *When the blue wave rolls nightly on deep Galilee."*

And ends with the majesty and power of God Almighty...

> *"And there lay the rider distorted and pale,*
> *With the dew on his brow and the rust on his mail;*
> *And the tents were all silent, the banners alone,*
> *The lances unlifted, the trumpet unblown.*
>
> *And the widows of Ashur are loud in their wail,*
> *And the idols are broke in the temple of Baal;*
> *And the might of the Gentiles, unsmote by the sword,*

> *Hath melted like snow in the glance of the Lord!"*

God's grace in saving Judah wasn't merely for Hezekiah; it was all a part of His ultimate plan to keep the line of David intact that He might one day extend His salvation and grace to all mankind through Jesus Christ his Son (2 Kings 19:34).

At the beginning of this chapter we read Psalm 136. Look at this psalm once more. Verses 10-22 specifically speak of all the trials God brought His Chosen People through. And yet, were the Israelites perfect? Did they always get it right during their years in Egypt, in the wilderness, and beyond? No, they didn't. We can see that while they tried to be His Completely, sometimes they succeeded and sometimes they failed. We see the wonders and signs God did in their midst and often ask the question, "How could they lose faith in God when they experienced those things *firsthand*?" The power of the plagues, mighty waters parting, manna and quail falling from heaven, water to quench their thirst, great walls tumbling before their eyes, the Promised Land before them, the death of a giant adversary, fire from heaven, and so much more! How could the Israelites still fall? It is because they were just like us, were they not? Their everyday struggles, fears, weaknesses and sins were waging war against their faith. Hezekiah was great because he lived within the bounds of God's commandments, he sought the Lord's will and good pleasure, and he did it with all of his heart. Whether the subject is Hezekiah, the Israelites, or us it works the same way. If we begin to live outside the bounds of God's commandments, if we fail to seek the Lord's will in the things we do, and if we only live with half-hearted devotion, we will have the same result as the Israelites. We, too, will falter in our faith.

Chapter 10 – Having a Heart that Trusts in God's Grace

Although the time of miracles has passed due to the death of the apostles (Acts 2:43; 8:14-24), God is still working. Amazing things happen everyday! And though now He uses natural means to show His power and glory – He is still there. His works in verses 4-9 are lasting evidence in ages past and for ages to come of His mercy, His lovingkindness, and His grace toward us. We can trust in God's grace today because we have the evidence of His grace for the Israelites, an imperfect people. This same grace He offers to us through His Son if we will only commit ourselves in love and obedience to be His Completely.

> "Give thanks to the Lord, for He is good,
> For His lovingkindness is everlasting.
> Give thanks to the God of gods,
> For His lovingkindness is everlasting.
> Give thanks to the Lord of lords,
> For His lovingkindness is everlasting.
>
> "Who remembered us in our low estate,
> For His lovingkindness is everlasting,
> And has rescued us from our adversaries,
> For His lovingkindness is everlasting;
> Who gives food to all flesh,
> For His lovingkindness is everlasting.
> Give thanks to the God of heaven,
> For His lovingkindness is everlasting."
>
> (Psalm 136:1-3, 23-26)

Questions for Further Study

1. What similarities do you see between the worshippers God seeks in John 4:24 and the attitude and practices of Hezekiah in 2 Chronicles 31:20-21?

2. In our times of distress we know we should seek comfort from the Lord first, but who do we often find ourselves seeking comfort from before we go to God?

3. How does it make you feel to consider that God's preservation of Judah wasn't for Hezekiah alone, but it was for your own salvation through Christ?

4. List ways you can show God how grateful you are for the gift of His grace.

5. *Bonus Question:* In the classic movie *7 Brides for 7 Brothers*, Millie considers naming her new baby daughter a Bible name like Hannah, Hagar or Hephzibah. Who is Hephzibah?

CHAPTER 11 — *Yours* COMPLETELY

King Josiah — HAVING A HEART THAT IS FULLY DEVOTED TO GOD MEANS:
Having a Deep Love and Respect for God's Word

2 Minute Decompress — Breath slowly in and out three times. Read Psalm 119:105 followed by this song:

> "O God, You are my God
> And I will ever praise You.
> O God, You are my God.
> And I will ever praise You.
>
> I will seek You in the morning.
> And I will learn to walk in Your Ways,
> And step by step, You lead me.
> And I will follow You all of my days."
>
> (Rich Mullins)

From Ponder to Pen — According to Psalm 119:105, how does God lead you "step by step"? Have you been letting Him do that in your life? Why or why not?

KING JOSIAH'S STORY IS FOUND IN:
2 Kings 22:1-23:25 and 2 Chronicles 34:1-35:27

Chapter 11 – Having a Deep Love and Respect for God's Word

What were you doing between the ages of 16-26? Probably the typical things... going to school, maybe to church camp, playing sports, hanging out with your friends, working a job or going to college, possibly getting married and starting a family. Were you reigning over a kingdom? Probably not.

Josiah is one of the kings of the Divided Kingdom that brings about a great deal of curiosity for me. I just can't help but try to imagine what it would have been like to be eight years old and wear the crown. What kind of craziness is that?! I shudder to think of that much power being granted to an eight-year-old today. I have an eight-year-old and the only crown she wears is Elsa's bejeweled plastic crown as she dances around the room singing songs from the Disney movie, *Frozen*! As for having power, well she is the youngest child. She spends more time bending her will to her older sister's than knowing what it's like to be the boss! Then again, I have a typical American eight-year-old. And times were much different when Josiah was a child.

JOSIAH'S EARLY LIFE

Although he was just a boy, Josiah wasn't without his advisors to help him in his royal duties. It seems that Hilkiah the high priest was a help to him in carrying out his obligations and very likely served as a counselor to him as he grew, similar to the chief priest Jehoiada's role for King Joash.

We don't have details of King Josiah's everyday life – i.e. who his friends were, what they did, how he was educated, what he liked to do for fun, etc. Yet, we know that these things were a part of his life, as they are everyone's life - only the details are different!

We read in 2 Chronicles 34:1 that Josiah became king when he was eight years old. At 16 years old he sought the Lord to do his will (verse 3). This can probably be compared to many of us in our teen years feeling the call to obey the gospel and making the decision to be baptized into Christ to follow Him all of our days. We are old enough to understand who Christ is, what He did, what our response should be and the importance of making that decision versus not making it. As with Josiah, growth and deeper understanding come in time. Josiah's decision to seek the Lord is evidence of the teaching and training that was going on in his life while he was young. Let that be a lesson to us, as parents, to give spiritual guidance to our kids while they are young, so that when that time of decision comes they will be ready and wanting to make it!

In 2 Chronicles 34:3-7, we read that at 20 years old Josiah saw the sin that Judah had been wrapped up in and began to purge Judah and Jerusalem of its idolatry. True to the prophecy given to Jeroboam in 1 Kings 13:1-2, "He burned the bones of the priests on their altars" (verse 5).

Hear – Ponder – Apply

In 2 Chronicles 34:14-30, Josiah, at 26 years old, was faced with three opportunities. One opportunity led him to another, which led him to another, and to another. Choices would have to be made to continue to seek the Lord or to follow his own path. Upon hearing the Word of God King Josiah was faced with a choice – Disdain or Hear? And he would be faced with another choice – Disregard or Ponder? And then again, faced with another choice – Disobey or Apply? What makes this section of Josiah's story remarkable is that with each opportunity, he chooses wisely to have a heart that is fully devoted to

Chapter 11 – Having a Deep Love and Respect for God's Word

God and follow in His ways. Let's dig further into King Josiah's life and learn of the importance to Hear – Ponder – Apply.

HEAR

Clearing the land of idolatry was great, but as the workers were bringing the money out of the temple, Hilkiah found the book of the law of the Lord given by Moses. He gave it to Shaphan the scribe, who in turn brought it to King Josiah and read it before him. What did Josiah do? Did he disdain Shaphan's efforts? Did he turn aside in anger? Did he absentmindedly listen and then turn his attention to more pressing matters? No!

Josiah heard the Word and his reaction was strong and immediate! Verse 19 says, "When the king heard the words of the law, he tore his clothes."

How often do we speak to our kids and say, "Do you hear me?"

"Yes, Mom, I hear you."

"But, are you *listening*?" As parents, we know there is a vast difference between hearing with your ears and hearing with your mind and heart.

PONDER

King Josiah heard the Word of God that was read to him with his ears we know. However, we also see the evidence that he heard the words with his mind and heart. He obviously had a deep love and respect for God's Word. He recognized its power and importance. By tearing his clothes he showed great anguish for his neglect. He mourned and humbled himself before God. He knew that what the book was saying, as God's people, they were not doing. I wonder if, as their leader, he felt guilt for forsaking God's Law. He knew that the abandonment that began with past kings of Judah (not to mention Israel!) had provoked God's wrath against them. So Hilkiah and King Josiah's other appointees went to a prophetess named Huldah to find out what the Lord said regarding this situation. In 2 Chronicles 34:22-25 we read of their punishment for not obeying God. Then following, in 2 Chronicles 34:26b-28 we read of God's mercy on Josiah.

> *"Thus says the Lord God of Israel regarding the words which you have heard, 'Because your heart was tender and you humbled yourself before God when you heard His words against this place and against its inhabitants, and because you humbled yourselves before Me, tore your clothes and wept before Me, I truly have heard you,' declares the Lord. 'Behold I will gather you to your fathers and you shall be gathered to your grave in peace, so your eyes will not see all the evil which I will bring on this place and on its inhabitants.' And they brought back word to the king."*

God wants us to have a deep love and respect for His Word. He will punish those who fail to obey it (John 12:47-48), but He has mercy and forgiveness on us when we repent (Ephesians 1:7). If we truly are His completely we will have a deep love and respect for His Word. That love and respect will bring us to repentance when we, like Josiah, come face to face with our sin.

APPLY

In 2 Kings 23:1-20 we see King Josiah applying God's Word in two ways: he makes a covenant to follow God's Word again with all their heart and soul and he begins making more active reforms to clean up the abominations and idolatry in the land.

2 Corinthians 7:10 says, "For the sorrow that is according to the will of God produces a repentance without regret, leading to salvation, but the sorrow of the world produces death." King Josiah had sorrow that was according to the will of God. We see that his sorrow produced repentance – repentance that didn't just take place in his heart, but repentance that bore fruit that proved it was real! He didn't just **hear** the Word. He didn't just **ponder** the Word. He took it all the way and **applied** the Word. Those three actions joined together show us how Josiah had a heart that was fully devoted to God.

MAKING A CLEAN SWEEP

When Josiah wanted to purge the land of Judah of the abominations and idolatry against God, he didn't just do it halfway, he made a clean sweep. Like the old saying goes, "If you're gonna go, go all the way!" 2 Kings 23:4-24 lists out all of the things that King Josiah did to make a clean sweep of the land of Judah – it turned out to be quite the task! But, his efforts brought him praise from God at the end of his life. King Hezekiah is paid tribute in the Bible as being one of the best kings of Judah. But as great as King Hezekiah was, he did not compare to King Josiah. Even in spite of his youthfulness, Josiah is praised as being *the best* king of Judah. Why was he the best?

1. He was the best because he was fully devoted to God. His devotion to God was evident in that he loved God with all this heart, soul and might (2 Kings 23:25).

2. He had a deep love and respect for God's Word (as is shown in his reaction to the reading of the lost book of the Law).

3. He set himself to obey what was in the book (the lengths he went to remove idolatry in the land show this).

4. He influenced the people of Judah to do the same (in vast contrast to Jeroboam who led the people of Israel further into sin!).

Such great praise from God Almighty is found in the words of 2 Kings 23:25, *"Before him there was no king like him who turned to the Lord with all his heart and with all his soul and with all his might, according to all the law of Moses; nor did any like him arise after him."*

Do we have the same deep love and respect for God's Word?

In this chapter we see Josiah doing three vital things to show he was completely devoted to God: Hear- Ponder- Apply. Those are three things that we, as Christians, must challenge ourselves to do. We have opportunities to *hear* God's word every Sunday and Wednesday (and sometimes other days in between). Are we taking those opportunities? We don't have to wait for someone to find a lost book of God's Word and read it to us. The majority of us have our very own that we can read any time of day or night! Do we find ourselves disdaining Bible reading? Or do we take the opportunity to "Hear"?

And what do we do from there? Do we choose to disregard the things that we have read and heard from God's Word? Or do we *ponder* those things – really think about them and their meaning for our life? If we love God with all our heart and soul and might as Josiah did, we will challenge ourselves to let God's Word go deep into our hearts.

However, just as hearing is not enough, pondering is not enough either. We must also *apply* those things to our lives. We must see our short comings, our sins, and rededicate ourselves to doing better and trying harder to not fall into those sins again. As we see in the story

Chapter 11 – Having a Deep Love and Respect for God's Word

of King Josiah, neglecting to do the right thing is just as spiritually dangerous as willfully falling into sin. When necessary, we must make a clean sweep of the sin in our life. Clear it out and destroy it. Remove it as fully and as thoroughly as Josiah did in 2 Kings 23:4-24.

Let us take Josiah's example to Hear – Ponder – Apply.

> There are 176 verses in Psalms 119 and nearly every one speaks of God's Word. We see these terms used: *Your Law, Testimonies, His Ways, Precepts, Statutes, Commandments, Judgments, Your Word, Ordinances.* How great is God's Word!

We are not under the Old Law now; we are under the Law of Christ, the law of Liberty (James 2:12). We, in the Christian Age, should have the same love and respect for God's Word today that those (like Josiah) under the Old Law had in the time of the Old Testament. Although it is a lengthy chapter, take time to read through Psalm 119 and think about how you can have a deeper love and respect for God's Word in your life.

A Prayer to be His Completely

"Let my cry come before You, O Lord;
Give me understanding according to Your word.
Let my supplication come before You;
Deliver me according to Your word.
Let my lips utter praise,
For You teach me Your statutes.
Let my tongue sing of Your word,
For all Your commandments are righteousness.
Let Your hand be ready to help me,
For I have chosen Your precepts.

I long for Your salvation, O Lord,
And Your law is my delight.
Let my soul live that it may praise You,
And let Your ordinances help me.
I have gone astray like a lost sheep; seek Your servant,
For I do not forget Your commandments."

- Psalm 119:169-176

Chapter 11 – Having a Deep Love and Respect for God's Word

QUESTIONS FOR FURTHER STUDY

1. When you look back on your life between the ages of 16-26, how would you gauge your devotion to God and His Word? How have you grown or diminished in your faith over the years?

2. How much have you grown as a Christian in faith and knowledge since the time you were baptized into Christ?

3. Why do some people feel they have to know "everything" in order to be baptized? What is the danger in this belief?

4. Go back and look again at the four reasons that Josiah was the best king of Judah. Could these examples be applied to you in your life?

5. Choose a verse from the Bible that you feel you need to work on in your spiritual life. Challenge yourself to read this verse everyday for a week, each day meditating on it and trying to hear – ponder – apply.

CHAPTER 12 — *Yours* COMPLETELY

HAVING A HEART THAT IS FULLY DEVOTED TO GOD
What will be Your Legacy?

2 Minute Decompress — Breath slowly in and out three times. At the beginning of Chapter 4 we read the chorus of the following song by Steve Green (2006). Take a moment now, to read through the complete lyrics.

> We're pilgrims on the journey of the narrow road
> And those who've gone before us line the way
> Cheering on the faithful, encouraging the weary
> Their lives a stirring testament to God's sustaining grace
>
> Surrounded by so great a cloud of witnesses
> Let us run the race not only for the prize
> But as those who've gone before us, let us leave to those behind us
> The heritage of faithfulness passed on through godly lives
>
> After all our hopes and dreams have come and gone
> And our children sift through all we've left behind
> May the clues that they discover and the memories they uncover
> Become the light that leads them to the road we each must find
>
> Oh may all who come behind us find us faithful
> May the fire of our devotion light their way
> May the footprints that we leave, lead them to believe
> And the lives we live inspire them to obey

(http://www.songlyrics.com/steve-green/find-us-faithful-lyrics/#7gDC01eFHqhIGDVk.99)

Chapter 12 – What will be your legacy?

From Ponder to Pen – Imagine you can hear what is said at your memorial service after you pass from this life. What do you imagine will be said of you and the life you have lived? Will those you love be able to say you were fully devoted to God?

Throughout the pages of this book we have studied various kings of the Old Testament, trying to answer the question, "What does it mean to be fully devoted to God"? Kings like Hezekiah and Josiah set a good example of how to live our lives in complete devotion to God, while kings like Ahab and Jeroboam set poor examples and by contrast showed us what *not* to do. Although we studied only nine of these kings in depth, each king of the United and Divided Kingdoms left a legacy behind. Reading through the pages of Bible history, we see that each king's life is summarized, either at the introduction of his reign or at his death. Saul, David, Solomon, Jeroboam and Rehoboam are the exceptions to this type of abbreviated summary, as much more detail is given by God about each of these kings throughout their reign and life.

Take the time to read through the summary of the lives of each king of Israel and Judah. It is surprising how few words it takes to reveal a person's heart for God and obedience to God or lack thereof. We may not have the power as God does to see into a person's heart, but deeds to others and obedience to Him reveal much about devotion. Matthew 7:15-18 reveals this truth as it gives a warning against false prophets. The subject matter may be different, but the principle remains the same. *"Beware of the false prophets, who come to you in sheep's clothing, but inwardly are ravenous wolves. You will know them by their fruits. Grapes are not gathered from thorn bushes nor figs from thistles are they? So every good tree bears good fruit, but the bad tree bears bad fruit. A good tree cannot produce bad fruit, nor can a bad tree produce good fruit."* Were these kings completely devoted to Him? Some were. Others were not. But each one, no matter how brief his reign, is a reminder to us that one day each of us will pass away and leave behind a legacy that will reveal our devotion to God. Consider that as you read through the following verses.

SUMMARIES OF THE KINGS IN 1 AND 2 KINGS, FOLLOWING REHOBOAM AND JEROBOAM

- 1 Kings 15:1-3 Abijam, son of Rehoboam (Judah) Many of the kings are compared to King David and his devotion to God or to Jeroboam and his leading Israel to sin
- 1 Kings 15:9-11 Asa (Judah)
- 1 Kings 15:25-26 Nadab, son of Jeroboam (Israel)
- 1 Kings 15:33-34 Baasha (Israel)
- 1 Kings 16:8, 13-14 Elah (Israel)
- 1 Kings 16:18-19 Zimri (Israel)
- 1 Kings 16:25-26 Omri (Israel)
- 1 Kings 16:29-30 Ahab (Israel)
- 1 Kings 22:41-43 Jehoshaphat (Judah)
- 1 Kings 22:51-53 Ahaziah, son of Ahab (Israel)
- 2 Kings 3:1-3 Jehoram/Joram, son of Ahab (Israel)
- 2 Kings 8:16-18 Jehoram, son of Jehoshaphat (Judah)
- 2 Kings 8:25-27 Ahaziah, son of Jehoram (Judah)
- 2 Kings 10:28-31 Jehu (Israel)
- 2 Kings 11:1-3, 20 Athaliah (Ahaziah's mother usurps the throne of Judah)
- 2 Kings 12:1-2 Joash/Jehoash (Judah)
- 2 Kings 13:1-2 Jehoahaz (Israel)

Chapter 12 – What will be your legacy?

- 2 Kings 13:10-11 Jehoash (Israel)
- 2 Kings 14:1-3 Amaziah (Judah)
- 2 Kings 14:23-24 Jeroboam II (Israel)
- 2 Kings 15:1-3 Azariah/Uzziah (Judah)
- 2 Kings 15:8-10 Zechariah (Israel)
- 2 Kings 15:13-14 Shallum (Israel)
- 2 Kings 15:17-18 Menahem (Israel)
- 2 Kings 15:23-25 Pekahiah (Israel)
- 2 Kings 15:27-30 Pekah (Israel)
- 2 Kings 15:32-34 Jotham (Judah)
- 2 Kings 16:1-3 Ahaz (Judah)
- 2 Kings 17:1-2 Hoshea (Israel)
- 2 Kings 17:7-23 *Why Israel was sent into exile in Assyria*
- 2 Kings 18:1-3 Hezekiah (Judah)
- 2 Kings 21:1-2, 16-17 Manassah (Judah)
- 2 Kings 21:19-24 Amon (Judah)
- 2 Kings 22:1-2 Josiah (Judah)
- 2 Kings 23:31-32 Johoahaz (Judah)
- 2 Kings 23:36-37 Jehoaikim (Judah)
- 2 Kings 24:8-9 Jehoaichin (Judah)
- 2 Kings 24:17-19 Mattaniah/Zedekiah (Judah)
- 2 Chronicles 36:13-16 *Why Judah was sent into Babylonian Captivity*

So, what have we learned?

In each chapter we have learned what it means to be His Completely – a harmony of both our heart and our obedience to God.

- *King Saul* showed us that in order to be completely devoted we must learn to be completely content in the life that God has given us.
- *King David* showed us that we don't have to live with guilt every single day. We all sin, but we all have a path to forgiveness if we will cultivate a repentant heart.
- *King Solomon* showed us that we have to have a heart that is undivided in our service to God, lest we find ourselves only partially devoted.
- We dug a little deeper into the *Divided Kingdom* and learned some valuable history to keep in mind while studying the kings.
- Through *King Rehoboam* we learned the value of carefully considering the things that influence us.
- *King Jeroboam* was a man who was self-serving throughout his life and through him we learned how important it is that we be a God-serving people.
- By the example of *King Jehoshaphat* we learned that if we will take pride in the ways of God our lives will reflect a complete devotion to Him.
- *King Ahab* taught us, through his poor example, the importance of acquiring spiritual clarity that we might clearly see our spiritual life as God would see it.
- *King Hezekiah*, in the conflict of his human flaws and his desire to serve God, showed us the blessing it is to be able to trust in God's grace.
- And *King Josiah*, from his very youthfulness to adulthood, showed us that the only way to know God's will for our lives and how to please Him is to have a deep love and respect for God's Word.

Each of the kings that we have read and studied about were teaching something about how to live for God. They may or may not have even realized it at the time, but they were setting an example. For some kings, their example helped their son to keep the Israelites strong and faithful to God. For other kings, whether it was a conscience decision or not, their example showed their successor how to lead the Israelites further and further from being fully devoted to God.

LEAVING OUR OWN LEGACY

We are all at this very moment setting an example with our lives. We are writing our legacy with every word we say, with every choice we make, with everything we do! What a concept to wrap our minds around! Yet, it is true! Is it not? We each set an example for others to follow in our attitudes and actions. Through our work, worship, words and conduct we are teaching others what it means to be fully devoted to God. We will all leave a legacy behind when we depart this earth. And when that day comes, what will people say of us? What will our friends and co-workers say? What will our church family say? What will our children and grandchildren say? More importantly, what will God say of us as we stand before His throne? I pray that each of us will take the lessons learned from this book, plant them in our hearts that they might grow and flourish in our lives, so that one day our God will be able to say of us that we were *His Completely*.

QUESTIONS FOR FURTHER STUDY

1. What kind of fruit do you believe you are producing in your life?

2. Who is following in your footprints? Will your life lead them closer to God or further from Him?

3. What is your impression as you read through the legacies of the kings, especially in light of James 4:13-15?

4. Of all the kings who we studied in this book, which one gave you the most encouragement? Why?

5. Which king challenged you to improve something in your walk with Christ? In what way?

Chapter 13 – Additional Study Aids

CHAPTER 13 — *Yours* COMPLETELY

ADDITIONAL STUDY AIDS

Trivia OF THE *Kings* REVIEW

(Can you answer these without looking back at the Table of Contents or Chapters?)

1. Our studies of the kings have showed us that devotion to God has two parts. What are they?

2. Can you be fully devoted to God if you only have one part, but not the other, in your life?

3. Which king, though he prayed for understanding, foolishly allowed his love for foreign women to carry him away from God?

4. King _____ showed us that a repentant and contrite heart brings about God's forgiveness and mercy.

5. Which king of the United Kingdom struggled with being completely content?

6. The two tribes of the Southern Kingdom were referred to as _____.

Chapter 13 – Additional Study Aids

7. The ten tribes of the Northern Kingdom were referred to as

8. King Rehoboam taught us that we have to be careful about who _____ us because they just might lead us to be devoted to something other than God.

9. King Rehoboam was counseled by two groups of people about how to treat the Israelites. Which group did he listen to? Was that a wise choice?

10. Which king was known for leading Israel away from God and devised in his heart his own way of worship?

11. Which king was said to do what was "good, right and true" in his work for God?

12. What nation was known for its cruelty to its captives and forced other kings to pay tribute to them?

13. Which king taught us that having a heart that is fully devoted to God means being God-serving instead of self-serving?

14. What was the Fun Fact from *Seven Brides for Seven Brothers*? Hephzibah was the mother of _____ who was the son of King _____.

15. King Ahab saw it as a trivial thing to walk in the sins of which king?

16. The tribes of Israel were taken into captivity by which nation?

17. Which King taught us that when we are faced with trouble or uncertainty in our lives our prayer should be "O my God, I do not know what to do, by my eyes are on you"?

18. Who became king at 8 years old and later sought the Lord to do His will?

19. The tribes of Judah were taken into captivity by what nation?

20. What three things does King Josiah's example challenge us to do when reading God's Word? H_____
    P_____ A_____

Chapter 13 – Additional Study Aids

WHAT DOES IT MEAN TO BE *Saved by Grace*?

A Study of Ephesians 2:1-10

(Additional study for Chapter 10 - Fill in the blanks using the text taken from the NASB)

WHO WE WERE WHEN WE WERE OUTSIDE OF CHRIST (VS. 1-3):

1. Dead in our _____ and _____
2. Walked according to the course of this _____
3. Walked according to the _____ of the _____ of the air
4. Walked according to the _____ who now works in the sons of _____
5. Formerly lived in the _____ of our _____
6. Indulged the desires of the _____
7. Indulged the desires of the _____
8. Were by nature children of _____
9. Were just the same as _____

LIST GOD'S ATTRIBUTES FROM VERSE 4.

1. He is _____ in _____.
2. He has a _____ _____ with which He loves _____.

WHAT THE FATHER DID FOR US (VS. 5-6):

1. He made us _____ together with _____
2. He saved us by _____
3. He _____ us up together with Christ
4. He made us sit together in the _____ places in _____ _____

WHY DID HE DO THAT (VS 7)?

1. So that He might show the _____ _____ of His _____.
2. So that He might show His _____ toward us in Christ Jesus.

SO THAT WE MIGHT BE SAVED (VS. 8):

1. By _____
2. Through _____
3. Not of _____
4. It is the _____ of God
5. Not a result of _____ (so that no one may _____)

Chapter 13 – Additional Study Aids

IN OUR NEW LIFE (VS. 10):

1. We are His _____

2. We are created in _____
   _____ for good works

3. God prepared long ago for us so that we would
   _____ in them

    GREAT LOVE

    RICH IN FORGIVENESS

    A GIFT OF GOD

FOUND IN **C**HRIST

    EVERYDAY WALKING IN OUR GOOD WORKS

5 *Great Lessons* FROM THE LIFE OF *Hezekiah*

1. HE HELD FAST TO THE LORD IN TRUST AND OBEDIENCE (2 Kings 18:5-7).

> "He trusted in the LORD, the God of Israel; so that after him there was none like him among all the kings of Judah, nor among those who were before him. For he clung to the LORD; he did not depart from following Him, but kept His commandments, which the LORD had commanded Moses. And the LORD was with him; wherever he went he prospered..."

2. HE DEPENDED FULLY ON GOD FOR HIS SALVATION (2 Kings 19:14-19).

> "Then Hezekiah took the letter from the hand of the messengers and read it, and he went up the house of the Lord and spread it before the Lord. Hezekiah prayed before the LORD and said, "O LORD, the God of Israel, who are enthroned above the cherubim, You are the God, You alone, of all the kingdoms of the earth. You have made heaven and earth. Incline Your ear, O LORD, and hear; open Your eyes, O LORD, and see; and listen to the words of Sennacherib, which he has sent to reproach the living God. Truly, O LORD, the kings of Assyria have devastated the nations and their lands and have cast their gods into the fire, for they were not gods but the work of men's hands, wood and stone. So they have destroyed them. Now, O LORD our God, I pray, deliver us from his hand that all the kingdoms of the earth may know that You alone, O LORD, are God."

3. HE SOUGHT THE LORD IN HIS TIME OF SICKNESS (2 Kings 20:1-3).

> "In those days Hezekiah became mortally ill. And Isaiah the prophet the son of Amoz came to him and said to him, "Thus says the LORD, 'Set your house in order, for you shall die and not live.'" Then he turned his face to the wall and prayed to the LORD, saying, "Remember now, O LORD, I beseech You, how I have walked before You in truth and with a whole heart and have done what is good in Your sight." And Hezekiah wept bitterly."

4. HE DID WHAT WAS GOOD, RIGHT AND TRUE IN HIS WORK FOR GOD   (2 Chronicles 31:20-21).

> "Thus Hezekiah did throughout all Judah; and he did what was good, right and true before the LORD his God. Every work which he began in the service of the house of God in law and in commandment, seeking his God, he did with all his heart and prospered."

5. IN THE FACE OF TRIAL, HE REMEMBERED THAT GOD WOULD BE THERE TO HELP FIGHT THE BATTLE (2 Chronicles 37:7-8).

> "Be strong and courageous, do not fear or be dismayed because of the king of Assyria nor because of all the horde that is with him; for the one with us is greater than the one with him. With him is only an arm of flesh, but with us is the LORD our God to help us and to fight our battles." And the people relied on the words of Hezekiah king of Judah."

Other Publications from Yeomen Press

Publication	Author
We're All Wounded (for women)	Debbie Kea
40 Years on the Second Pew (for women)	Debbie Kea
Complete in Christ (Colossians)	Glen Elliott
Just Christians (for evangelism)	Gary Witcher
Victory (A study of Romans)	Gary Witcher
The Lion and the Lamb (Revelation)	Gary Witcher
New Testament Commentary (one volume)	Jim Sheerer
NT Commentary on CD-Rom	Jim Sheerer
Collected Popular Articles and Lectures	Everett Ferguson, PhD
Women in the Church (for women)	Everett Ferguson, PhD
A Handbook on Leadership (for servants)	Edited by David Duncan
The Fullness of Time (God's perfect plan)	Gerald Pinson, PhD
The Book (How we got the Bible)	Gerald Pinson, PhD
Reaching New Levels of Faith	Curtis Hartshorn
My First 52 Days in Christ (new Christians)	Curtis Hartshorn
The Essence of Revelation (Revelation)	Curtis Hartshorn
Backwards (for young adults)	RD Erickson
Tradition: From A to Z (doctrine)	Lee Peters
Christianity Applied (20 pdf lessons)	Jim Sheerer & Charles Williams

New Testament Commentary e-pub version at www.shelfwise.com
Quantity discounts available at yeomenpress@gmail.com
www.yeomenpress.com

Acts 2:38 – Peter *said* to them, "Repent, and each of you be baptized in the name of Jesus Christ for the forgiveness of your sins; and you will receive the gift of the Holy Spirit." (NASB)

Yeomen Press exists to share the gospel of Jesus Christ with the lost in order to save souls from sin, death, and hell.

Yeomen Press

Cindy Sue Baker's Bio

Cindy was born and raised in a small town in Kansas. She attended both York College and Oklahoma Christian. She and her husband, Aaron, have two young girls named Kaela and Melia. In 2004, Aaron and Cindy both graduated from the Bear Valley Bible Institute of Denver. From 2005 to 2012 they were missionaries in the country of Vanuatu in the South Pacific. They love the Vanuatu people and try to return every year to help teach and encourage the Christians living there.

Currently, Aaron and Cindy work with the church of Christ in Foristell, Missouri where Aaron serves as the minister. Cindy teaches women and children's classes and is involved in various aspects of the women's ministry in the congregation. In addition to her homemaking and church-work, Cindy also works part-time as a Chiropractic Assistant.

Cindy has self-published two books about overseas mission work: Lord, Give Me Pretty Feet (2010) and March On: My Year in the Vanuatu Bush (2012). She also has had a few of her articles published in Christian Woman Magazine.